Weddings in Paradise

A Guide to Getting Married Away from Home

Denise N. Fyffe

Weddings in Paradise

A Guide to Getting Married Away from Home

Advice on how to plan a destination wedding at a
fantastic island getaway, like Jamaica, or in your
own country.

Table of Contents

Weddings in Paradise

Planning a marriage proposal and a wedding can seem to be daunting tasks. Nowadays, social media and online videos apply even more pressure because they are so elaborate, romantic, or original. You might even be consumed for months, thinking about where, when, and how to pop the question. Some people choose restaurants, birthdays, special gatherings, or just a simple walk on the beach to propose to their special person. Others go back to special spots, to both the groom and bride, to have their wedding ceremony.

No matter where you choose, you will have an incredibly happy fiancé, when done right. However, not everyone feels confident about planning a marriage proposal or a wedding because of the pressure and high expectations. No worries, this guide will provide you with many tips on how to propose and plan your wedding in paradise.

The Marriage Proposal

Imagine going down on one knee, asking the most important question you will ever ask and hearing an unfavorable response. This is not something you want to go through, so make sure you have an idea of how your special someone feels and what they are likely to say.

Most couples discuss marriages and their expectations, at one point or another in their relationship. Before you ask the big question, ask the small but important ones. Get an idea of how invested they are in the relationship, what they think, and whether they want to marry you. For some, this is obvious in their interactions and a discussion may not even be warranted.

After taking that first step, some of the anxiety should ease. It will be easier to take the next step and begin planning the details for a wedding, such as how and where to pop that special question.

It's All in the Details

So, you know they want to be with you forever and you with them, but do you know their ring size? Do you know what rings they might prefer? Or, even whether they want to have a ring at all? Where can you purchase an engagement ring? How much can you afford, or do you need to save up? What is the cost of wedding rings in your area? Should you purchase it online or at a store? And do you know what to look for when purchasing a diamond ring?

These questions should be answered before you go ring shopping. If your special someone does not require extravagant surprises, then, in this case, you can take them ring shopping, and let them pick out their ring. If you are on a budget, ensure you have an affordable selection waiting for your perusal; but, make sure to do your research and prep work. Furthermore, you can ask their friends and family about their likes and dislikes, or subtly get answers from them over the course of your relationship.

Most importantly, you need to understand the four C's of buying a ring. This refers to the cut, carat, color, and clarity. There are thousands of ring options that look like diamonds, so beware, if this is your preferred choice. Your girlfriend or boyfriend might not actually prefer a diamond, which may be rare. So, find out what type of stone, and setting your loved one may prefer.

After you have bought the ring, get it insured. This has been a hard and painful lesson learned by many couples. Stones can fall out, and rings can be stolen or lost. So, get ring insurance and this ensures that you have a safety net to replace it if the ring or the stone goes missing.

Also, when the time comes to pop the question consider a bit of tradition. One traditional practice, that is always cherished and respected, is asking for the hand of your future spouse from their father, parent or guardian and getting their blessing. This sets an even stronger foundation for your relationship with your in-laws in the future.

Finally, remember to go down on one knee when proposing. This is considered one of the most romantic gestures. Your future fiancé might even get flustered and start crying but remain composed and execute your plans. If possible, have someone record the moment for posterity; using a photographer is better than using a Smartphone. If that is not an option get a camera. You can ask your friends, family or a close co-worker, to help on that day.

Though, in many cases a cooperative stranger can sometimes be your best choice; at restaurants the staff can help also. Remember, plan out your proposal, and do something that you know will excite and make them incredibly surprised, happy, and emotional. The more emotional, the better the pictures, video, and memories for later; enjoy and celebrate the moment after.

The Wedding Date

It's time to make the ultimate decision, when to keep your wedding? This is a major contemplation for most couples. You try to make it suit your convenience but sometimes you are impeded by the availability of your most important guests. You also try to consider the best time of the year, and your favorite time of year. If you live somewhere that's impacted by rainy seasons and hurricanes then you will also need to adjust your date to avoid these, as best as humanly possible. Do not be pressured when you get engaged. Take time to think about what you want and what will be feasible for all involved. The pressure involved in setting a wedding date, often makes some couples elope.

There are other considerations. For example, do not keep your wedding in the winter if you absolutely hate the cold. If you sweat a lot, do not keep it in the sweltering summer months. Brides, think about the plight of the groom and his friends in those buttoned up suits. Also, think about a time of year that you absolutely love. If autumn or spring is your favorite time of the year go with one of them. Make sure you give your guests more than adequate time to plan and prepare for the joyous occasion.

If you want to get married on the beach, then select one of the sunnier seasons; the summer being the perfect option. You can also take your wedding party to a nice destination, like Hawaii, Maui, or Jamaica. If you prefer a garden wedding, then the summer or spring is a lovely time as well. At these times you will be able to enjoy the lovely array of blooming flowers and if flowers are your primary focus and you absolutely must have a particular type, then use this to guide your choice wedding date.

Also, holidays are not exactly the best time to have a wedding celebration. The costs involved with planning this type of wedding may be more than you can manage. Vendors might take advantage of you then. Your guests might also find it extremely difficult to attend a wedding during the holidays. Also, try to avoid the lent season, and Easter as they might also have some cultural or religious practices. However, if you want to have a holiday wedding ensure that you consult your guests and choose a long weekend that can accommodate them.

Remember, weddings tend to have some of the most disastrous things happen if they aren't planned properly. Do not plan your wedding in a rush, consider all your options and research the location if you are unfamiliar. Else, it might be a prime opportunity to be on America's funniest wedding videos. Furthermore, if you live in an area that has a lot of snow, think about how your guests will travel and for those guests who are coming in via flights, try to plan around the possibility of flight delays due to poor weather conditions.

The Four Seasons

A wedding is one of the biggest occasions in your life, especially for a bride to be. From the planning of the proposal and it's acceptance, the games will be on. Therefore, ensure you pop the question at the right time, so that you can still catch up on the sporting events you love. While your bride is consumed with wedding plans you can enjoy your games, including the NFL playoffs.

Keep in mind though, that your fiancé will pull you into some of the wedding planning activities. Therefore, you probably should invest in a pocket size device, download a sports app or bookmark a sports streaming site, so that you are prepared for all the interruptions that will be coming your way. Also, while you are stocking up your fridge with all the beers and liquors to enjoy your sporting event, you should also learn a little more about the time of year you get married. This will help you to subtly guide your future wife in picking the best date for a wedding, and still be able to catch all your games.

Summer

Avoid summer weddings, which are exceedingly popular for weddings, all the sun and beautiful flowers appeal greatly to many brides. So, understand that there is a season called 'wedding season.' This is to women, what NFL is to men. The downside to having a wedding at this time, is that everything will be at a premium price; venues, food, transport, flowers, and even wedding planners. If you can afford it, and your bride is dead set to have it then, I guess you don't have a choice, do you? If not, try to nudge your bride to another season. One of the pros is that those traditional tropical honeymoon destinations like Jamaica, and Hawaii will be off peak season. This means that you will save on honeymoon expenditure and you both can enjoy a destination with an all-year summer feel.

Fall

Consider a fall wedding, which are not prone to the 'summery,' hot conditions, which can be very stifling and one of the best torture methods for grooms in suits. Your photographs will thank you for choosing this time of year. Also, it is still off season for the best island destination locations. Plus, you will have more time, and can make arrangements for the children - if you have them. This will be easier as they should be in school. The biggest disadvantage to you, is that it is prime NFL season.

Winter

The winter season goes from November through to February. This is where the pros and cons flip. You will be able to access cheaper wedding services. Locations will be available, and offered even at discount rates, because fewer people are getting married at this time; the same for catering services, and all other wedding services. Another benefit is that you can kill two birds with one stone, as family would typically be gathering around for the holidays; therefore, you could combine the celebrations. Furthermore, you will be more likely to remember your wedding anniversary.

Spring

Spring is another peak season for weddings and a wonderful time for the 'bridal fever.' It is perfect in terms of temperature and weather. The variations of flowers are also numerous. However, keep in mind the holy, Lent and Easter holidays, as your guests may celebrate this or have certain practices during this time of year.

The Wedding Budget

The first step when considering a wedding budget is to know what your finances are; whether it will be a loan, savings, parents, or another source. Then, you should set a maximum limit, that you will not go over and a minimum limit. You will need to research, make calls, and visit locations to find out about possible costs. Call the hotels, or vacation travel agency, you can go online as well. Visit several locations, ask relevant questions about packages, and discounts so that you are informed.

To minimize costs, some people wear the attire of family members, especially brides. They opt for their mother's wedding dress and make alterations if necessary. You can also call on your friends and family members to help with miscellaneous expenses, to cut expenses. Items such as decorations, party favors and the invitations, can be done at get-togethers. Doing so will reduce the amount of wedding stress you encounter. Do you really need a wedding planner? This can also take a chuck of your budget, the money you save by going online and downloading wedding lists, and resources, can be used towards your honeymoon or food.

Financing the Wedding

There are many things that are necessary for a successful wedding. Some you can live without, some you cannot. First, the bride's most important concern is her dress. For an item that will only be worn on one day, it has the potential to start wars and break engagements. This item can cost thousands of dollars and may consume a large part of the budget. Not to mention other items like the wedding cake, caterer, food, beverage, flowers, tuxedos, entertainment, and transportation. In planning this event, you must also consider the miscellaneous costs that will be incurred while planning for a wedding. This is why it's important to have a wedding budget and stick to it; so that it guides you when faced with tempting situations that cause you to overspend.

Stay on course! This might be like carrying water in a basket, but it is possible. Capture all the different expenditures in your wedding and research what the cost will be, taking into consideration fluctuations until the time you pay your bills. Add a couple hundred or thousand dollars to that, just to have a buffer, in case incidentals are added up. When you have a total, go back over your list, and remove the things you can do without and can't afford.

Additionally, most businesses may require down payment. For some people, you might have to consider getting a loan if you do not have the funds saved to pay for all the upcoming expenses. Consider payment terms, the payback term, and your new joint expenses, plus other factors such as the interest and principal payments. When you have identified the best loan option, create a wedding account, and pay all wedding expenses, only, from this account. Once everything is paid off, and the honeymoon is over, start repaying your loan promptly. Depending on the type of gifts, and your use for them, you can use those to assist in covering your wedding costs. Remember, the priority is to begin your newlywed life, debt free. Getting a loan is a last resort.

The Splurges

One of the most expensive events in our lives is a wedding celebration. Couples must be extra careful and prudent; especially in tough economic times and cut back on spending as well as staying within their budget. Having a lavish wedding is not as important as staying out of debt and beginning your marriage debt free. If you stick to your plans and find creative means of getting what you want, then you can have a dream wedding without breaking the bank.

First, you will need to sit down with your partner. Identify areas of the wedding that you must have and that you are willing to spend overspend on; these are generally the big-ticket items like the wedding dress and even your wedding pictures. Once you have done this, also identify things that you will cut back spending on, which are not so important. You can reduce your spending on areas that you can do for yourself or ask assistance from family members and friends. This can be with the invitations, cake, decorations, or transportation. The things you decide on will change depending on what is important to both the groom and the bride.

One area that can take a huge chunk of the wedding budget for many people is the location or venue of the wedding reception: or both the ceremony and reception. The aesthetics of the location and ambiance is especially important for the occasion. It should be a setting where you can have beautiful pictures and fond memories to look back on later. If that reception site specializes in weddings and has a coordinator, this takes a lot of the stress from off the bride and groom. It gives you more time for other projects on your list. Such a site will negate you having to consider smaller wedding budget expenditure on chairs, tables, decorations, and cake. This will really draw down on your expenditure at the end of the day. Make sure to make a down payment or the full cost if you have made your final decision.

Another area where you may want to make wedding splurges is the photography and videography. This, to most, is the most important aspect. Capturing the excitement, dances, exchange of vows, speeches, and happiness on your guest's faces, is a necessary part of a wedding. Finding a good photographer ensures that you will have beautiful and quality shots to cherish for later. If you also have a videographer, then this doubles your chances of getting those memories captured and in the eventuality that something happens, have a backup. Many video cameras today, also allow you to do snapshots.

Next, the food and drink are another area you might consider overspending on. However, if you have friends or family in this business that can assist, call on them for their assistance. Wedding food doesn't have to be bland and boring; it can be very tasteful and quite appealing to people's appetite. The rings will also require you to overspend sometimes, especially if the bride falls in love with a particular one. Although, if you decide to cut costs, you can use a family heirloom, like a grandmother's ring or other important family member's cherished wedding ring.

The Guest List

The guest list is always a cause for concern when planning a wedding. The total number of wedding guests directly affects your wedding budget. Therefore, many couples want to include only friends and family. But, when you have a plus one, things may really start to get out of hand. Therefore, planning your list will take thoughtful consideration and you will need to be very firm.

Furthermore, seating is always a major consideration as well. You will, at some point put together people who do not know each other. Therefore, you want to ensure that they have things in common to keep a conversation going. You will need to visualize or map out a seating chart. Think about mixing people who can carry a conversation, and those who are avid listeners. You might also want to think about keeping some family members together, like that of the bride and groom, mixing them, so that they can get to know each other. Often family members only get to meet each other, and maybe for years at a time, at weddings. This will allow them to catch up and reconnect. You may also consider having a kiddies table at your wedding reception.

If you are not having large tables, you can have smaller intimate settings; where the table seats no more than four to five and some two to three persons. This may depend on the type of wedding, theme, and the wedding reception location. Having intimate settings allows you to have a wider array of friends, especially if they are planning on carrying a date. This will negate you having to think about where to seat people and who they will talk with. Of course, you might want to keep a head table. This is a typical and traditional wedding practice, and a family table as well.

Often, couples must think about people who have interpersonal issues or family feuds. They must keep in mind whether to put Uncle John to the north and Aunt Jane to the south. If your parents are divorced, place your mom as far away from your dad as you can. Another consideration is how to mix or place your single and married friends. You may not want to be too conspicuous with this. The best time or opportunity to mix up your guests is when you are planning a buffet meal. Here you can play around with whom to invite; like some old friends or new associates you would like to get to know better.

Finally, you will have to revisit the wedding seating arrangements on numerous occasions. Maybe because of people who can't attend the wedding, the list being increased by your parents inviting friends, or for any number of reasons. But, leave some room to maneuver when planning the seating for your reception, just in case you have extra people showing up.

The Wedding Vows

It is important to take care of every detail that is involved with planning a wedding; after all, leaving one thing out can cause extremely bad repercussions on the day. Who needs that stress? With time, patience, and proper planning every aspect of a wedding can go on without a hitch; but do not forget the true meaning of the event. People get caught up in the wedding celebration, the wedding reception, the entertainment, the food, and the wedding venue. Though weddings are beautiful and have warm memories, when planning the couples may forget about the most important thing of all and that is your partner and the commitment you are making on that special day.

You should not forget why you are having a wedding ceremony in the first place. Remember the person who will stand across from you at the altar; the person who you will vow to spend the rest of your days or life with. That person is why you are having a wedding in the first place. Compared to your wedding vows, all else fades. When you make the effort to not only write original vows, but memorize it for that special person, it does mean so much more. Take the effort you put into planning the entire wedding event and pool some of that effort into making that person remember what you said and promised them.

This is an exciting and thrilling time in your life. You are filled with bubbly emotions for your fiancé, use those emotions to create your vows. You might even have some deep emotional thoughts about how they make you feel and how important they are to you. One of the most special aspects of a wedding ceremony is hearing the bride and groom exchange vows, which they have written.

For many people upon becoming engaged they wish to write their wedding vows, but they have some difficulty doing so for many reasons. To many it is incredibly important that they express, in their own words, how they feel about their partner and what they think about them. If this is your experience, under that the process doesn't have to be difficult and labor intensive, neither do you have to be the next Shakespeare to do so. With the required time, energy, and dedication you can get this task completed with little or no problems.

You may want to talk to your fiancé and the person officiating the wedding about writing your own vows. Note in some places it might not be allowed. But you won't know until you ask. In speaking with your spouse, you will find out if this is something you both wish to do. After doing this there are a few things you may want to consider; this may involve a little trip down memory lane.

When did you realize you loved your fiancé? Identify things you really adore about them and jot down your most cherished memories of being together. What significance does your marriage to them have? Do you think there will be changes once you are wed, or will things stay the same? And you may want to mention what type of wedding you wanted when you were younger.

After identifying these things, it will make writing your vows so much easier. Next, you will have to think about whether you will write your vows together or separately. Many couples write their vows together because they are starting a life journey together. If so, find a quiet place where you both will not be interrupted. Put away all distractions including your phone. Gather the supplies you will need like pens, pencils, and paper, or computers and laptops. Consider setting a time limit for how long you will do this each day and what your goal end date will be.

You can write in separate rooms if you prefer; and furthermore, another way to write your vows is by writing it as a letter. Remember the questions you answered before? You can use them to do help this process. Also, you can include songs, quotes, movies, or other elements that are special to both of you. You might have chosen to share your pieces once you are finished, or not. If so, this might get emotionally intense, and laughter and tears are allowed. If you wrote letters, you could choose the best sections to use as your vows and including any wording that's necessary for the service.

Don't forget, two different vows are needed, the bride's and the grooms. The last step is to present them to the minister, pastor, or officiant for his seal of approval, be open to his suggestions as he has been doing this for a while. You can write your vows, with the intention of surprising your spouse on the wedding day; just keep in mind the guidelines previously mentioned. Practice, practice, practice and get comfortable with what you have written.

The Traditions

There are many traditional practices that's often incorporated in weddings. They can be family traditions, religious traditions or even the standard cultural traditions. Wearing an elaborate gown, the bride carrying floors, getting married in a church, having the father give away the bride, having something old, new, borrowed, or blue.

The wearing of a veil is also traditional practice. The veil is worn in assorted styles and length. They can be quite simple of vary extravagant. This piece is almost equally as important as the dress. Before current trends, the veil was worn over the face of the bride for the entire ceremony, until being lifted by the groom. Many believed this was allowed so that evil spirits would be shunned. As time progressed many women have allowed their father, who walked them down the aisle, to lift the veil and reveal them to their future husband.

The kissing of the couple is seen as 'sealing of a deal.' In the past, this signified binding the contract of marriage. Now it is done, as a visual show of affection, by the couple, towards each other. The procession down the aisle is another tradition. So too is having your father walk you down the aisle, as a bride. Some include both the mother and the father. In some cases, the father might not be alive, or there might be some other issue. In this case the bride will choose another family member or a close and respected friend.

The exchange and presentation of the rings symbolize the union and symbol of their love. Both the groom and then the bride will put the ring on each other's ring fingers. Before the advent of the diamond ring, people used grass or hemp, braided to fit on the finger representing everlasting love. However, around the fifteenth century people started using the diamond wedding band. Additionally, the throwing of rice is a symbol or wish of fertility. Now some couples use other creative measures, like blowing bubbles, flower petals, or birdseed.

The wedding reception also has many traditional practices as well. From the first dance of the father and bride to that of the married couple; also, the throwing of the bride's bouquet are popular traditions. This came about, in England, when the guests used to take things from the bride as a sign of good luck. In order not to be disrobed the bride threw her flowers. Finally, cutting the cake goes back to when they used to break the cake over the bride's head. The cake being tiered is yet another English custom.

Beach Wedding dress

The location of the wedding is almost as equally important as the wedding itself. The venue sets the mood of the ceremony and gives a general sense of the love felt in your relationship; of course, this will be aided by the wedding decorations. But many wedding venues, or locations for wedding, need no extra help, they can simply take your breath away and give the bride and groom many good memories for years to come. Having a wedding on the beach can be a majestic idea especially with a beautiful and breathe taking back drop.

Picture crystal clear white splashes of water hitting the rocks and beach. Picture a beautiful sunset and smell the clean scent of the air; all these things will add to the ambiance of a romantic occasion. More and more couples are opting to have their weddings on the beach than in a prissy chapel, with traditional garbs. Having your wedding on the beach also frees you from having to weigh a wedding dress that weighs a ton. Brides can play around with several designs and millions of colors, and patterns. If you wear a long gown on the beach, it will not stay clean for long. You run a significant risk of having a dirty, muddied, designer gown; and no bride wants that on her wedding day. You will also have to tug and lift the train more often than if you were any place else, because of the dirt and sand. This will surely detract from the happy and festive feelings you should be having, and you will likely be more irritable.

Destination wedding gowns are just as beautiful and competitive as traditional wedding dresses. These can be easily located at the designer stores or bridal boutiques.

Many boutiques and shops specialize in these types of dresses. Some designers who make these wedding dresses include Jessica McClintock, Alfred Angelo, and Impression Bridal. They create the perfect top of the line designs. If you are having difficulty finding these dresses in a store, ask the assistance of a store clerk or assistant. They will be happy to aid you in making the right selections that fit your style and wedding theme.

These wedding dresses can then be accessorized easily. First, you would not be required to wear a veil; wearing a veil on the beach will have you fighting with the wind, and this may be very distracting. If you desire something in your hair, you can wear a floral headpiece or even flowers arranged nicely. Because of the windy condition, consider holding your hair back from your face in lovely hairstyle. Make sure you select comfortable shoes that you can wear safely on the beach, especially in the sand. Do not wear heels; it can be a treacherous undertaking. Think about incorporating sandals, elegantly designed flip-flops, or ballerina slippers. Numerous couples have gone without their shoes on their wedding day.

Informal Wedding Dress

The wedding dress is considered the centerpiece of the wedding. Most people come and leave such a ceremony with the whispers of about the dress on their lips. They discuss the design, the designer the length, the train, and how beautiful the bride looked in it. Little girls often fantasize about their weddings to their prince charming and what dresses they will be wearing. Some have picture books, and scrap books with things they want to include in their wedding when they grow up. Therefore, the wedding dress is a big, big deal. Many brides prefer simple, elegant, and casual weddings. But they do not know how they are going to execute their wishes. Casual weddings can be just as special and elegant as any formal wedding.

If you are thinking about a garden wedding, a casual sundress may be a great option. This could be in a cotton or linen design. These dresses are especially perfect for casual summer weddings. They can be any length you desire but are mostly kept short. Sundresses are flattering to the figure and are also exceptional choices for a beach wedding. Another excellent selection is a floor length maxi dress. You can select an off white or white dress; in any time, material you desire. There are limitless options for the patterns and design on the wedding dress, leaving the bride looking and feeling very whimsical.

Suits are another great option. They are an excellent choice for people who have been married more than once and might be over the fluffy big gown idea. The Jackie O classic look or a practical pant suit in any color including white, can be worn to a day or evening wedding. This is a viable choice for weddings being kept in courtrooms. You can change your attire for a dress at the reception.

Strapless gown, made of satin may appeal to some brides. Strapless gowns can compliment your upper body, especially your shoulders and back. This timeless option can even be worn in a fitted design, showing off the figure of the bride. Mid-calf, tea length dresses are sometimes chosen by the bride. Accessorized by kitten heels and pearls and you will have a very elegant looking bride. This also makes for lovely attire at a casual wedding. It is suitable for a Sunday wedding, with a brunch reception. It is also perfect for garden weddings. If you are considering a beach wedding, choosing a tea length gown, will minimize your risk of falling and dragging on your wedding day. You will have less sand to contend with.

Being comfortable on your wedding day should be a primary concern. You do not have to be strapped in, sucked it, tied into, or feeling unnecessary pain on the most important day of your life. Designers are now making it possible to wear different dresses that will match your wedding theme.

Something Old

"Something old, something new, something borrowed, something blue", all and sundry knows about this age-old saying. To make sure of happiness in the marriage, it is believed that a bride should have these things for good luck. These items are often included creatively in the wedding. Weddings are filled with the invocation of many traditional practices. Those passed down from one generation to the next. Families also play a vital role in these traditions, passing on heirlooms and other little trinkets.

The bridal gown is often a prime example of this tradition. Often mothers of female family members will pass on a wedding dress, and it might be the brides something old, or something borrowed and on occasion something blue. Brides need to ensure that they do not wear these gowns out of guilt but because they want to, and it fits the overall wedding theme. Jewelry is another accessory that can fit the tradition, and often is. This may include earrings, pendants, broaches, watches and even the wedding ring itself. Men have been giving their brides the heirlooms or rings of their mothers or some other relative. For those who do not have these items handed down in their family; you can visit internet selling sites such as eBay and Amazon to find real treasures. Visiting the antique store in your area is another good option. Remember stick to the style of your wedding.

One thing that will take little effort is having 'something new.' Between the bridal shower and other gifts, plus, your own shopping you will have covered your bases in this regard. Remember, your something new can be anything, including lingerie. The same applies for your something borrowed. This can be jewelry, dress, anything from friend of family especially if you have admired it yourself for quite some time and your wedding day would be the ideal day to get it. If your female relatives still have their garters, this might be an opportune time to borrow it.

Be careful on selecting what your 'something blue' will be. You do not want it to be distracting, gaudy or clashing with the wedding theme. A new trend is using people, like the maid of honor or mother dressed in blue, as that tradition. Other items that can be used are underwear, jewelry, hair pins, shows, bouquets and handkerchiefs.

Many people are not aware of the "a silver sixpence in her shoe" tradition. Finding this silver penny may be impossible, therefore you can use a dime or penny or depending on your country some local coin currency. But you may want to check auction sites, local pawn, and auction shops for a silver sixpence. Having things that symbolize tradition, in a wedding can be a very fulfilling experience.

Wedding flowers by season

Flowers make a wedding. Couples tend to use their favorite flowers and include them in the wedding; and by couple, we mean the bride. Roses, lilacs, sunflowers, and many other types are used to decorate the tables, used as center pieces, used as the bouquets for the bride and bridesmaid, and used as decoration in every and anywhere conceivable. They create the ambiance, and this can be anything you wish. However, they can be expensive if you are thinking of using out of season the best advice, is to always use flowers that are in season, at the time that you are getting married to minimize your expenses. Else you will have to factor in the huge shipping and delivery costs into your budget.

A wedding in the fall has the enormous potential to many different flower types. The color spectrum is marvelous during this time of year. You will have many flowers in reds, oranges, yellows, and browns. This will also dictate your wedding theme and color choices. Many people's favorite flower, the rose, is in bloom during this type of year. Having a wedding with this season's color will be extremely beautiful and often breathtaking, when done right. Other flowers flourishing at this time of year includes the hocus pocus, terra cotta, red berlin, leonidas, star 200, black magic, and confetti.

The spring offers you a choice of light colored and fluffy flowers. They make for a lovely, pretty spring wedding decor. These flowers are great for bouquet, centerpieces, and decorations. The colors that are available during this season include soft greens, pale yellow, baby blues and tender lavenders. Tulips, daffodils, and roses will make excellent bouquets and garnishes. Choose your flowers wisely, you can even mix the flowers for an even more dramatic effect. Yellows and often soft greens will work perfectly. When selecting the bridesmaids' dresses, and their color, also think about the color of the flowers you will be using and how best it can complement the dresses. The same goes for the groomsmen.

The most popular time for weddings is summer; everyone loves having a bright sunny setting for their special day. At this time of year, it offers a vast array of flower choices. You can go for almost any color scheme or decor. The color choices will be bright and fitting to your environment. Roses are one flower that is available almost all year round, and if you wish you can include them into your summer wedding; they are a traditional choice. The popular color choices include yellows, reds, and oranges. Your wedding can be set to a minimalist aesthetic or an extravagant flair. Whatever time of year you decide to have your special event, make sure the flowers are available during that season, it will be more cost effective and easier on your pocket.

The Usefulness of Wedding Magazines

Planning a wedding is an exciting event. Many women look forward to doing this their whole lives. Some even take it on as a career as coordinators and wedding planners. However, not many brides or couples are informed about how to plan a wedding or what are their options. Many who can afford the expenditure will hire wedding planners, and this can get very costly. Even though they might have the experience, and have done this many, many times; having a planer is not cheap. You might turn to friends and family who have been through the experience and might have an idea at what to do. This is a cheap alternative as you won't have to pay them for their services. But the final decision is yours and it is best to become informed about the possibilities, so that you get all that you want.

Wedding plans do not finalize themselves overnight. They take time and research. This cannot be done in each day. You will have to locate bridal shops, flower shops, decorators, or supply stores, visit venues, and many other treks will have to be done before your wedding day arrives. Whether you use the help of others, you will still need to visit some of these places. Leaving everything to others, should never be an option.

Reading wedding magazines can be immensely helpful in making your decisions concerning your wedding. Anything to help ease the stress and tension that might arise during this period, is always a plus. Magazines, that specialize in wedding arrangements, designs and gowns, are the best to refer to. These have editors and writers who focus on this industry and research materials that are applicable to a cross section of readers. They will have issues that deal with gowns, venues, planning, decorations, and other things to do.

Some magazines carry feature wedding gowns and bridal dresses exclusively. They will have pictures of all unique styles, colors, and designers. As a bride you will be able to explore the type of dress that suits or appeals to you and learn what traditional, casual, and trendy styles are in season. Magazines sometimes list where wedding gown designers and stores are located. These magazines also provide information on honeymoon destinations, the cheapest rate, and the best travel plans. They may also carry articles on the dos and don'ts of the wedding night, and other relationship advice. The magazines are not the gospel of wedding planning, though they provide solid advice at times. You might want to read them to just get general ideas, or on what to do. You can ask friends to read through with you and discuss your ideas with your friends and family.

The Groom

The Wedding Tuxedo

The attire of the wedding party should coincide with the location and mood of the wedding. Choosing your wedding attire is particularly important occasion. This will be the lasting memory in many people's mind when they talk about your wedding. Many times, people from the wedding party dread the decisions of the bride and groom as they might choose some ghastly designs. Usually, the emphasis is on the bride and the bridal party, the colors chosen and the design of the gowns. Brides often invest an immense amount of time searching for and trying on dresses, while grooms usually take a straighter forward approach. However, sometimes the decision is not so easy in selecting the perfect wedding tuxedo.

Many weddings are based on themes, while others are more traditional. The traditional weddings are easier to select a suit for, as men tend to go with simple, classic cuts and designs. Their decisions are often to look good but not taking away from their bride. The tuxedo must always compliment the brides dress and make the man look polished and smart. For a themed wedding, the tuxedo should fit the selected theme. You will have on this suit for a particular length of time, therefore choosing a comfortable and weather friendly one is especially important. You should not look to wear a wool suit in summer or a light cotton ensemble in winter. Light airy materials should be selected in summer, especially if the wedding will be held on the beach; white is also preferred for a beach wedding. Your wedding tuxedo will be casual depending on the time you host the ceremony.

You can incorporate your individual style into your wedding tuxedo selection. Do not be overly flamboyant as to be ghastly and distracting. You can show your style in the accessories you wear, like cuff links, ties, vests or even shoes. Sometimes it's best to keep it simple. You should select a wedding tuxedo in a timely manner, not a week before the wedding. You might need to make alterations, or even have a special suit made for you. Having the suit fit to your comfort, not too short, not too long; it should be perfect as your wedding pictures are forever. The sooner you have a suit the more time you must get the accessories that will compliment it.

Some men choose to rent their tuxedos. There are a few things to consider when dealing with your tuxedo selection process. First, the suit might not fit very well; hence, you must spend time finding the perfect fit which may not exist. Secondly, a tuxedo is not expensive especially when compared to the bride's dress. This means that men can more likely afford to get a custom-made tuxedo that will fit all the criteria described before. In addition, getting the perfect shoes, for the perfect suit is also important.

Wedding Day Tips

Many people who tattoo their skin have the areas that display the tattoo waxed or shaved; especially if it is very hairy, like their arm. Manscaping is a novel idea for some men; the thought of removing hair from places such as your chest, arm or back is just an intolerable thought. However, this might be very considerate if you plan to vacation on an island and strut your stuff on the beach. It will also be considerate to your new wife. Women shave, pluck, and wax almost every part of their body; men may consider doing this for some parts of theirs.

Removing hair is a serious contemplation for men especially those who are macho and are highly against it but will consider it for their spouses. If you are going to shave or wax certain areas, keep in mind the need to moisturize and use sun block to both protect it from sunlight and keep it moisturized. If you plan on venturing to the Caribbean, Jamaica, Honduras, Hawaii, South Pacific or any tropical area this is even more necessary.

Here is another great reason to remove unsightly hair. It will look horrible and repulsive on the beaches or in public. If you have back hair or an immense overgrowth of chest hair consider, waxing. Men, you should be even more tolerant of the pain as it does not last forever. Your newlywed wife will be very appreciative, receptive and might even reward you for your sacrifice.

A lot of people shave their armpits. Seeing a bushy forest from under a man's arm is truly a put off and might be a huge turn off, if you are planning on wearing tank tops on those tropical getaways. Another benefit is that, once removed, you will not have to worry about your odor or perspiration so much as the deodorant will be applied directly into your skin. The occurrence of sweat marks and stains on your shirts should also lessen. This act is both beneficial to you and your partner.

Removing hair from your man bits; now this is a tricky topic for some. You do not have to go as bald as a newborn baby. You have different alternatives, like just trimming. Remove the excess. If you choose to shave all off, then you must maintain it, as anywhere you remove hair, there will be stubble. This can give our spouse razor burn or chaff her skin.

Tanning is another consideration for those all white and milky men especially if you are coming from the colder regions. You might not want to glow when you visit the tropical islands. You don't have to do excessive tanning in tanning salons. You can choose to go to a spa and allow them to air brush you. Choose a nice shade that will compliment you and not make you look like an orange human.

Wedding Day Responsibilities

Wedding day responsibilities for the groom can vary. One of the first areas that a groom can help with is the paperwork. There is a lot of paperwork involved in preparing a wedding. Applying for a wedding license will kick off the list. Visit the respective department or ministry to get this done. You will also need to investigate about doing blood tests and doing travel plans.

If you plan to visit another country, you will need to find out the health requirements. You will need find out whether you will need to get shots and if there is paperwork you will need to get done. Some countries will require that you have a visa, so make sure to make your visa application in a timely basis. Ensure your passport is also up to date.

Another area of importance is including your spouse's name on financial documents and accounts. Make time to go to the bank and have her added. Some people may do this after the wedding ceremony to be safe. If you have wills and insurance policies take care of these as well.

Honeymoon is another event you can take care of. This can be elaborate to surprise and please the bride, or it can be as simple as booking a hotel in a Caribbean destination, that takes care of majority of the details. The attire for the groom's men will also need to be decided on; whether you will rent or buy. What accessories are need and wear to order or get them. Other areas you can assist with are the budget, guest list, invitations, and finance.

Doggie Best Man

Dogs are known as a man's best friend. Therefore, it is only fitting that they be included in the wedding in which they have been included in many. Winter, summer of fall there are many ways you can incorporate a piece or the very presence of your favorite canine at the wedding ceremony and maybe the reception as well. There are other ways you can have them included. Pictures placed at the reception, or even the wedding itself, and a brief mention of their involvement in your lives.

However, before all these decisions are made, you must answer a few questions. It is important to know the temperament of your pet though. It might not be wise to have aggressive or extremely shy pets at your wedding. They might cause more disruptions than you need. Can your dog be controlled around strangers? Does he whine, bark, or move around a lot? If he can be very cooperative, does the location you have chosen for your wedding ceremony and reception allow dogs? If not, how else can your dog be included? If he or she is allowed, what is the procedure? Do you have to pay a security deposit? Is it that he must be on a leash? Can he be carried, if small?

Now some of these concerns will be irrelevant if you are hosting an outdoor celebration and all you must be concerned about is how to include him in the celebration. Smaller pets are easier to manage and control. They can be held in the arms or carried in a basket by any member of the wedding procession. It is particularly important though that the animal be extremely comfortable and trusts the person who is put to care for them on that day. You do not want a friend or bridesmaid being nipped, bitten or worse. Remember animals are sensitive creatures and the slightest shift, if they aren't comfortable, they will react especially if not trained.

Some couples will ensure to get their canine friends suited out for the ceremony as well. There are tons of websites, stores and boutiques that cater to dressing your pets. You could choose simple accessories like bow ties, and tiaras. Alternatively, you may choose more elaborate costumes such as his own tuxedo, with a corsage or flower on his collar. Ensure to move it where he cannot be distracted by it. Pinkbellygifts.com is one popular website that provides wedding attire for your pet. You can get your florists to make them a wreath as well.

Ensure you have little necessary things to cater to their needs, like doggie treats, water, bowl, and a chewable toy. These will help to distract him and keep him fed and happy. Have an animal setter on hand if you will be going on honeymoon and there is no one else to care for him.

Themed Weddings

Having a beautiful wedding is all any bride ever wants. From the moment they were little girls, believing in fairy tales, or wowed by the sereneness offered by a beach; themed weddings can make all these dreams come through. Having a themed wedding can be a wonderful experience. Your guests will be awed by your chosen decor. If you do not decide on how, you want your wedding to look, you will default to the over-the-top princess wedding.

You should have a discussion with your groom to decide on what you both want for your island or Jamaican wedding. Do you want a casual beach or garden event with only family and friends? Do you want the extravagant gala, at an illustrious hotel, do you want to add adventure and have the event in an air balloon, the ocean or in a cave? Or do you wish to choose the location, where you both met? All these are considerations when planning a themed wedding because the venue you decide on might not incorporate a particular theme. For example, if you are trying to have a butterfly wedding in the underwater.

You cannot be a generalist when you are deciding on a wedding venue. You should be specific about the theme you wish to have. If your themed wedding is in a garden, how about deciding on whether you want a rose, dove, or butterfly wedding. This will help you when it comes to selecting decorations and in seeking permission from the garden about what you can do to the venue.

Brides are often industrious, even more so when they have the assistance of their friends and families. Bridesmaids can get together and have decoration making parties.

It is not difficult to make decorations and instructions can be found on the internet. This will make the themed wedding occasion even more special when you see how pretty your efforts are years to come. This can also make for fun memories in social gatherings in the future with family and friends.

When the wedding is looming, excitement fills the air. Choosing flowers, invitations, decoration, and a venue will give your ideas about how you want your wedding to look. Theme weddings are immensely popular now. They allow you to live out your fantasy wedding and have beautiful pictures that you can look back on. If you do not pin down a theme, you may end up with the typical fairy looking wedding, which is what most people have. You need something unique, that the bride, groom, and guests will appreciate, enjoy, and never forget. Therefore, get your bridesmaid together, find a wedding movie or clips and start planning. Make sure to note the unique features, decorations, and flowers that they have. This will help you in making your decision.

Choose a specific theme, do not be too general. Don't say you want a fairytale wedding, a Victorian wedding, or a garden wedding. The more detailed you are the easier your planning will be. For a garden wedding you could decide on a butterfly, rose or ladybug wedding. You could add different creatures to the decorations and make it very festive and representative of a garden in blooming with birds and butterflies. Then you can visit stores to get the specific decorations needed to create this. You may not find all you need in one place, as they may not stock a huge amount of what you need. But you can visit multiple locations and have friends help you too. Go to decorations, party, or costume stores.

Shopping on the internet is so much easier these days; especially if you cannot find all that you may need in one place. It offers the convenience of shopping at any time, and delivery come right to your door; so, no lugging huge packages or backdrops. If you have an idea in the night, it will be easy to get up and search for it. Finding what you want will not be a problem online, because there will be numerous options to choose from, with the ability to compare prices.

Your wedding favors can also, add to your theme; making it easier to put together. The decorations you put on the table, cake, and place settings help to build your theme, as well the type of linen, tablecloth, and backdrop. Being smart in the selection of your wedding favors will cause less stress in implementing your theme.

The other areas involved in the planning of your wedding can become distracting and overwhelming. Selecting a theme for your wedding and sticking to the plans set out, will reduce the headache involved. Remember to consider your dress and the dresses for the bridal party, the groom's men, and the guests. Make sure everyone knows what to expect at the earliest time, as their attire will add to the ambiance as well.

Adventurous Wedding Venues

Weddings are one of the most romantic events – especially an island wedding. Seeing two people saying their wedding vows, dedicating their lives to each other and pledging their undying love, it's so romantic. The ambiance, flowers, and colors all add to this atmosphere of romance. Another element that dominates in our minds when we think about romance is the location. The wedding venue is always a crucial factor. Many people chose traditional locations like churches and rent ball rooms. In recent times, people are exploring more avenues. Some chose locations that are even more memorable than the ceremony itself. Allocation should have a special or intrinsic meaning to the bride and groom. They should both attribute some occurrence of importance to this location. Many choose the place they met or went on their first date.

For the more adventurous sort, getting married in an air balloon is very ideal. They see this in keeping with the height of their emotions and love for each other. This is a popular choice. But for some, especially those with a fear of heights, it would be an awfully bad idea, although many may choose to get married in or on the sea. Deep sea diving weddings are for those who have a passion for the open sea. Many couples who do this share a common love of this environment and believe it is the romantic wedding location for them.

Keeping on the trend of nature, some couples may choose to get married in a cave. The reason for this may vary, but it goes back, to being one with nature, and feeling close to the ancestral ties. Stadiums, golf courses and arenas are another popular location. Many do this because they met there or are a lifelong fan of a particular theme. This goes back to the idea of choosing a location that both the bride and the groom love and have special memories there. More and more weddings are being held outside.

Many choose local parks, floral gardens, and country settings. These are exquisite choices that call for fewer decorations. Many parks and floral gardens will aid the couple in cutting costs on floral arrangements. Though the wedding will have to adhere to certain rules in order not to spoil or mar the natural flora and fauna. Beaches are one of the most popular choices. The sound of the waves, the feel of the wind and the majestic beauty that this locale provides, is coveted by many. A Jamaican wedding on the beach ensures beautiful wedding pictures, a semi-formal or casual choice of attire and a very relaxed atmosphere.

Your choice of wedding location should be a shared decision the groom and bride. They should feel a connection and want to create new memories there. Wedding locations should be chosen because they add to the romance of the event and will also be comfortable or accessible to your guests.

Beach Wedding Venues

The idea of having a wedding on the beach is extremely romantic. Both concepts alone are examples of romance and love; therefore, to combine both things should make for a very memorable and special affair.

Do you have a beautiful beach close to you? Then this can be an inexpensive location to host your ceremony. It will prove to very unforgettable for both you and your guests. For those who travel to Caribbean islands such as Jamaica, Aruba, Barbados, Cayman Islands, or St. Lucia; their wedding is typically set by the beach. Hotels and planners may work to decorate, provide seating, flowers and food that complement the setting. This makes for an even more romantic occasion. You may choose to even use those beaches close to home where you will have the opportunity to visit on occasion.

If you live on the Spanish, Mediterranean, or Greek coastline; these are equally great wedding locations. You can choose to have a traditional, formal, or casual affair. Having a beach wedding allows you the freedom of creating your own ambiance and feel. If you want a dance floor, jazz band,

and formal attire; this can be easily set up with your coordinator. And the relevant decorations, tents and flowers can create that type of atmosphere. It you are trying to stick to your own traditional practices and ceremony that is easily arranged as well. Ensure you communicate these ideas with your planner, and continuously go over the details and preparations to ensure things will go as you expect them to. The beach setting already guarantees a level of casualness about it. You can make your dress simple, wearing bikini tops and floral skirts or even simple gowns. Men can choose to wear khaki or nice shorts with simple shirts. The bridal party and groom's men should follow suit.

Ensure to inform your guests of the chosen wedding location and the expected attire. This allows them to prepare adequately for the ceremony. You do not want people showing up in formal attire if everyone else will be in shorts and flora dresses. Also advise them on the right shows; especially if you will not be on a solid foundation. Walking in heels on the sand can be an accident waiting to happen, and you do not wish to have anyone hurt on your special day. If you will be outdoors put contingencies in place to deal with anything unexpected, like rain. Make sure you have tents if a building is not close to the venue. You may not want your wedding, guests, chairs, tables, and yourself to be drenched our blown away. There are many funny blooper videos of this happening to couples. So, if you do not want a disaster on hand be ready.

Romantic Wedding Venues

People work hard at pulling of a magnificent event when they are planning their wedding. Brides tend to go all out, in bringing in different flowers, food, beverages and cakes. They try to find the best romantic wedding venues and caterers. All their efforts are to make their wedding celebration both memorable and romantic. Weddings take a lot of work and with the right venue it can be an even more romantic wedding. The meaning of a romantic wedding is different for everyone. But to all it is an expression and occasion for love. Many are wowed by the bride and bridesmaid's appearance, some the ambiance and decorations, others a mixture of all these things.

Depending on the bride and groom's tastes the wedding venue can be anywhere. Some are romantic locations like beaches and gardens, others traditional like churches and great halls, some adventurous like underwater or in a hot air balloon. All these locations tend to have special meaning or importance to either or both the bride and groom. Oftentimes, its places they have been together, where they first met, or have always wanted to have their ceremony. Back in the days, people would choose traditional locations like the church and city hall. Here families get together have a simple wedding ceremony and then go elsewhere for a dinner or reception. Now it is more popular to have the ceremony in some exotic and unbelievable venues.

Beaches are a popular wedding venue. This is highly romantic. The backdrop helps to create an atmosphere of love, warmth, and romance. Beaches are a casual, and the happy couple have the freedom to even transform this into an elegant, formal setting if they wish to. Most keep the semi casual feel and brides dress in sun dresses, skirts, or short dresses, and grooms dress in khaki, cotton pants or less formal suits. Going into the sea, is an adventurous venue option. Not many guests will be present, but it will be an interesting and memorable ceremony.

Caves are also a popular location. Couples may allow the natural look, or they can transform the setting with environmentally friendly decorations. Usually, couples who are into nature or Wiccan practices may opt for this location. A sporting arena, a golf course or baseball stadium is another popular choice. Many couples share their love for a particular sport; others might have met there or have gone there on many occasions. This is for the adventurous types, and often it is very romantic for very sentimental reasons. Couples have chosen to get married in many other locations. It is their memories, decorations of the love and experience of their friends and families that make these locations special. Romance can be whatever a couple makes it.

If you are having a terrible experience with a caterer who does not return you messages or calls, then you need to rethink your choice. No caterer is so busy that they do not have time, always, to speak with their clients answer questions, and make phone calls. This is the essence of good customer service and a method in ensuring repeat or word of mouth business. Taking weeks to respond to a client is a big sign that you need to rethink your choice and get a new caterer. They should never say they're too busy to respond to you. If they do, then that means they will not have the time, to manage your wedding needs when the time comes. Responsive and accessible wedding caterers will always have the time to manage their clients concerns.

Professionalism is integral in any profession. How you manage your clients, dress, answer questions and operate not only reflects on your business but it also says a lot about you personally. Showing up early or on time for appointments, looking smart and well-dressed is an always the best choice. Clients will appreciate the effort and note how professional that caterer is, and they will feel comfortable having them manage their business. This type of caterer will be prepared to show you portfolios and even have samples. They will not be pushy and overrun your desires for your wedding.

Wedding caterers should also understand of your need or thirst for wedding knowledge, and they should offer it up freely. They will be good businesspeople that make you feel comfortable with your decision and ensure you know as much as possible. Making an informed wedding choice is all that can be asked for from the bride and groom; that a few unreasonable demands are customary.

Caterers who have the professionalism will also be flexible in catering to your reasonable requests.

Wedding Reception Venue

A wedding is a joyous occasion. People come together to celebrate the union of a bride and groom. They eat, drink, and toast the newlyweds. But weddings take time to plan, and it can become incredibly stressful doing so. Often the bride will take on the bulk of the planning, and she may enlist a wedding planner to assist. Careful consideration is taken when planning a wedding reception. When there are difficulties, it is easier to categorize your tasks into groups. These may be food and drinks venue, entertainment, decorations, date and time and budget. Though a planner may have a network of people to rely on, in getting things into place, the final decision should be yours on the exact choices.

The wedding reception planning can take some serious considerations; especially as it relates to venue and food. But this takes does not have to be daunting. The first step is to find a location that the couple both agree on. When you are deciding on this, think about its accessibility and how easy it is for people to get to it. Can they accommodate the number of guests, and do they have experience hosting weddings? Check with the coordinators at the wedding location, that the date and time you have selected is available.

Another aspect of planning a wedding reception is the budget. Prepare a wedding budget and stick to it. Setting price line for individual expenditure items will save you in the long run. Shop around during the selection of the wedding venue and find out if the costs differ, for things like food preparation, entertainment, and wedding favors. These items, managing them separately, can really cut into your wedding budget unawares.

Once you have a wedding budget, it is time to set the menu. What type of beverages will you have at your wedding? Will you cater for non-alcoholics? How do you plan on serving the food? Will it be served by waiters or buffet style? What dessert options will be on the menu? Will there be more than two? Will you serve chicken or fish? What will be the entrée? Or what type of wine will you use for the toast? All these questions need to be addressed when planning your wedding reception meal. The best decision is to give people an option in each course, as you do not want them to be forced to eat something they don't like.

Once you have settled on food and drinks, your next consideration can be the wedding decorations. This helps to set the ambiance of the venue and the wedding reception itself. This is what your guests will remember for years to come. Keep in mind the center pieces for the tables, the number of tables, and chairs you'll need. You will also need flowers, candles, or streamers. These should not be random decisions or selections. Another area for consideration is entertainment and wedding music. You will need to select a DJ, band, or instrumental wedding band. The type of wedding music needs to blend well with the ambiance and setting.

Fall Wedding Invitation Ideas

The thought of planning each aspect of a wedding ceremony can be quite overwhelming. Getting a bridal gown, selecting a venue, doing a seating chart for your wedding, or even deciding on invitations require much patience, planning, and time. Weddings are an incredibly beautiful occasion. Filled with romance and enhanced by the ambiance; set in part by the decorations and colors. The first thing for such an event that your guests will see, is the invitations. This bit of paper will set the stage for your ceremony. It will inform them of the theme of your wedding.

Fall weddings can be unique and very memorable, if planned properly. The colors you choose will complement the season and leave your guests very appreciative. One of the first decisions in your planning process is ⸌ to decide on a theme and the colors; as this will be incorporated in almost every aspect of your wedding. Just selecting any old invitation and then on arrival your guests find a different theme, will make them feel uneasy, especially if they dressed to suit the theme.

For your theme, select a specific one; whether it is by the beach, in a garden or a church. Be specific. Then choose your colors that will be used in not only the decorations, table clothes but also the bridesmaids' gowns or dresses. You do not want to make rash decisions, make its not all the colors of the rainbow. You want your wedding to be unique, but you also want it to be remembered for the right reasons.

Another way to ensure a unique invitation is to make them yourself. To do this you can use a tree leaf design, paper, or a computer design template. Get some transparent paper and write the invitations on them. Invitations do not have to be bent, you can have a straight leaf invite as well, and make copies for your guests, printing on different papers. The computer is also another way you can design invitations, there are thousands of design possibilities in doing this. You will have the option to do classic, traditional, contemporary, or themed invites.

If you are using traditional colors of the season, like orange from the pumpkin you can incorporate this on white paper, using black ink. Images can be of hay bales, leaves or pumpkins. This can also dictate the invitation shape. They can be shaped like pumpkins, or leaves. Play around with your ideas, incorporate the things you like about the season, such as carriage rides. Think about the current fall colors or colors that you like; for example, baby blue. Picking your colors at the earliest times, allow you to have a specific idea for your theme, invitations, and decoration.

Beach Wedding Invitation Ideas

Wedding invitations are an important part of the wedding. This is the first thing that people will see and notice about the event. It announces to the world, about your union and it informs them of what type of wedding ceremony you will have; whether traditional, formal, contemporary, or casual. People go out of their way at times to get really elaborate and expensive invites when they can be done just as nicely by hand or with cheaper alternatives. Open your mind when it comes to choosing wedding invites or the format in which they are sent.

Remember one of the important aspects of your wedding is to stick to the budget, and wedding invitations can be quite pricey. If you are getting married in a luxurious tropical setting, you do not have to break the bank on invitations. Your cards can still be unique and beautiful, but in your price bracket. To avoid these ridiculous expenses, do not leave the sending out of invitations until the last minute. Make your selections early, to avoid mark ups from unscrupulous businesspeople who try to take advantage of you. Another advantage of having them early is that you can shop around. This will allow you to compare prices, bargains, designs, and other details. Salespersons will then be working to attract your money by giving sale or discount prices. Remember to shop online as well, as there are thousands of resources to choose from.

When you start early, you will be able to give timely consideration to your wedding theme. Your choice of invitation should inform your guests as to what the wedding theme will be. This will let them know how to prepare or dress. You will also have the time and opportunity to show the options to your fiancé and discuss which ones you prefer. This discussion could lead to a change in what invitations and themes you want. You will then be able to negotiate with the suppliers.

There are a few things you need to consider when selecting wedding invites. First the wording on the front of the card; this needs to be catchy and meaningful. Even though you have selected a design that appeals to you and will impress your guests, you need to have good words or sentiments in your card. You can choose to add your own words, use poetry and other romantic bits, apart from the details about the wedding. If you have a friend who is a writer, you can ask them to assist you in wording your invites and jazzing it up. People are retrofitting these invitations with unique things, like music. This will be quite fun and should immediately bring a smile to the face of the receiver.

Weddings are an occasion not just for sharing memories and celebrating with the bride and groom, but also of having fun. Having wedding favors is a traditional part of the wedding. It is how you thank your guests for making the effort to come out and celebrate with you. Having a wedding on the beach allows you to prepare and give your guests any number of fun favors. This will unleash your creative side. People will remember your wedding and if your favor can be used over and over, they will for years.

Thinking about the ocean and beach can generate many ideas. List the things that come to mind like boats, caves, rocks, sea water, shells, fishes, sandcastle, summer, kites, roman, the breeze and pirates. All these things can add to what your trinket or wedding favor will be. One idea is to have little miniature treasure chests, white shells from the sea or a little kite with the couple's wedding date, names, and picture on it. A replica of sand can be at the bottom of the chest, of sand, with the information written there as well. Include little designs like hearts, roses, and doves. This idea can be used as place cards as well, once they leave the wedding, each person will take theirs with them.

The chest can be large enough to hold a wedding photo, so that after the wedding the couple can send out snap shots that fit in them. Other photos of the bride and groom can also be used. The treasure chest can also have a small magnet or card. You can add beach scene pictures, or one of the couple seating at the beach sharing a happy moment. The couple can also include their vows or a romantic poem, on the chest, especially at the side. There are many ideas you can play with in designing and stocking your treasure chest.

Using seashells or giving little fishes in two, can be a nice idea for a beach wedding favor. This will symbolize your union. Include cards and pictures or even some feed for them. You can get big seashells and decorate them, add colors, messages, and the wedding information. You can also tuck something of interest inside the shell. Another idea is a pirate's scroll. This is an idea that you can play around with. Think about adding your vows or some fund memory. Play with the paper type, light translucent and of assorted colors. The scrolls can be in varying sizes. You can think about using miniature bottles to tuck them into. There are many unique beach wedding favor ideas that you incorporate into your wedding.

Summer Wedding Favor Ideas

People always throw away wedding favors, eventually, that they have no use for. You do not want this to happen after spending so much money on them. Your efforts and planning would have been for naught. But if you come up with ingenious and simple options; things that people can use on the day or even when they go back home, this minimizes the likelihood of them being added to the wastebasket. You can sit and discuss with friends and family who have been to many weddings; finding out what their best favor was and the worst. This is a simple and effortless way to generate innovative ideas.

Giving guests handheld a fan as summer wedding favors is a popular practice. These months are known for their unbearable heat, and if your wedding is held outside, it could be a simple solution to the problem of heat and coming up with an idea for favors. Fans are a casual as well as fun solution, and depending on the type of design, can translate to a casual or more formal theme. The wedding date, couples name, and other odd bits of information can be printed on the handle of the paper that makes up the fan. Putting the picture of the bride or groom can also be done. Oriental fans are a favorite choice of many. They will also be able to use the fan in other locations, at other times. If the fan is very sturdy, it can last for years and be a favorite of many people; possibly something they can take back at an anniversary celebration. You can also use manageable, small, motored fans that can be easily carried and fit in ladies' bags. These fans can also be embellished with silk, or lace.

For a long-lasting wedding favor, think about giving plants. People can use them to add to their garden, or place in their homes. You will have to decide on a plant that most people can manage, doesn't require a lot of care, and can be transplanted if your guests wish to do so. Or you can have a mixture of plants. They can be fruit or flowered plants. Many people are environmentally conscious and there are foundations and groups that can have packages for the replanting of trees in deforested areas. This would be a nice memento for the occasion.

Packets of seeds are another perfect, environmental summer option for weddings. Your guests will be able to take these and plant them in the fall, or even on the wedding day. Again, this can be done in gardens, or in areas identified for reforestation. You can add cards with little notes and other keep sakes if you wish with instructions for planting the seeds and what type of plant they are. You can choose seeds for your favorite flower or fruits.

Second Wedding, Gift Ideas

What do you get someone who is getting married another time around? This will call for a bit of creative thinking; whether it is a renewal of vows or another different marriage, persons at the point usually has the household items they need. The size of the gift may be of some consideration, but your friendship with the persons will dictate the type, size, and cost of the gift. Your friends will be understanding if you do not break the bank and give them another pricey item, if you did the first time. By also being a friend, you would have been more aware of their needs. Unlike someone who is a business acquaintance who would speed less on a gift and get a more generic item.

On the second or so marriage, either party would have already had many if not all the household items, that people usually get as wedding gifts. They would have furnished their place and live in a particular style. You may look at w couple things, to figure out what gift to give the. What are their hobbies? Who do they spend their evening doing?

What's their career? Do they like travelling? Di they like books? Do they like shows, sports, or live performances? These questions will guide you on the best gift to get them.

If either the bride or groom is into arts or culture, there is a variety of gifts you can get them. Paintings make for lovely wedding gifts. Art sculptures, clay pots, unique pieces, or even a piece from their favorite artists will make them extremely happy. Also, if they are into entertaining and socializing you could give them pieces to add to their bars, kitchen, or basements. To add an extra special touch, you can get them into shows, theatre, and opera and have them meet their favorite artists backstage; they will be totally ecstatic about your gift and probably never forget. You would be the toast of their get-togethers for many years.

You can also get them memberships that align to their hobbies. For example, baseball season tickets, annual pass to theme parks, annual membership to a wine club, cheese club or book club. You can also have service deliver a little gift for them on their first anniversary, many wine clubs do this. If you have an awfully close relationship with either the bride or groom, or both; you can think about getting them individual gifts. Jewelry is always a desired piece of any bride, so you cannot go wrong in getting that for her. It should be easier than you think if you have a close relationship with any of the persons getting married because you know what the need, want and desire.

For Including Doves

Prince, who is a singer, songwriter, and multimillionaire, from the 1980 did a song called, "When doves cry". We all know that this is not so, but these lovely creatures are symbolic of love and unity. Thousands of weddings have incorporated them because of this symbolism. Couples add in white doves into their wedding ceremonies; hoping that it adds meaning and says to their partner, how they feel about them. It also indicates to their guests how in love the couple really is.

People experiment with their weddings more and more. They believe in including the many facets that they as a couple enjoy, especially with the theme and music. They keep the older tradition of throwing rice and jumping the broom; but they have included new traditions more. Therefore, weddings now include doves, bubbles, and anything else the couple can think to add.

The use of dove is very varied. Couples come up with different methods of setting them free or adding them to the ceremony. The trend is to use white doves. They can be released usually at the end of the ceremony from the chapel or loft. They can be released just before the couple drives off, or even after they say the I dos, depending on the wedding venue. The release indicates or represents the couple branching out into the world and starting a life together.

The reference to doves can also be included in the ceremony. This can be stated by the minister, priest, or officiator. He or she will draw reference to the symbolism, or it can be included by the couple in the vows, especially in the exchange of rings section. The decision as to when these references are made, or when to release the doves, lies with the happy couple.

You also need to consider the holding areas or cages for the doves. There are many ways to incorporate them, and how to display them. They can be kept close to the venue or ceremony area; just if they won't be a distraction or noisy. You can think about the color or type of cage to put them in; whether white, gold or silver. You can have a handler there who will see to their food and comfort needs. Because of what they symbolize your guests will be touched and many awed by their presence and inclusion into the ceremony.

When where and how to include the doves, does not have to be complicated. The couple can decide whether to include them in your nuptials, at the reception or after the nuptials. You can also dictate the number of doves to release. This can be two or more; and reference can also be made to this in the ceremony.

Weddings are beautiful events; hosted at some of the loveliest locations. Many couple set the date of their ceremony up to a year ahead. This gives them time to set their plans, scout locations, and get funds together. If you work with a wedding planner they are already seasoned enough to guide and make this process much easier, hence you will have less stress to deal with. Have you ever been to a wedding that has been decorated to suit that season? They are extremely, beautiful and fitting.

It is important to give yourself time in planning a wedding. The advantage is that you can scout venues and observe them, in the season you plan on getting married. If you are thinking about churches, halls, or grand rooms they might have some lovely alternative decorations or fixtures up already. You don't have to have a huge decoration budget if you shop around wisely. Ensure to ask about the decorations that they have and look at them if possible.

Weddings held at the New Years, Christmas season are fortunate to have places that are already decorated with lights and other ornaments. Make sure you ask them; their decorations will still be up after January first. If so, get that in writing, so that you will have no surprises. If you are that far ahead, visit the location the previous year, to see what you will be getting.

Many people have beautiful homes and gardens that suit the type of wedding you want to have. How about trying this type of location? You can enquire of that friend or family member, and I am sure they would be happy and honored to host the ceremony there. Same as before, visit the location, if you can, in the season which you plan to have the ceremony. If possible, you can plant flowers there before; so that they can be in bloom by the time you are ready. Spring is a lovely time to have a ceremony and many people may opt for parks but getting or booking one might not be as easy as you think. Hence asking your friend or family permission to use their residence is an easier, less stressful alternative.

Are you thinking about a summer wedding? Eyeing your favorite beach? Thinking about having the waves and coasts as a stunning backdrop? Summer weddings offer all this. You will have to ensure that the setting has what you need, or that you will purchase this for your decorations. Ensure that they suit the locale and the theme of the wedding. Palms are a lovely addition to a casual beach wedding. Destination weddings, especially if coordinated by a hotel or wedding planner, have the added benefit of taking on that responsibility.

Weddings in the autumn are every colorful, with the food and decorations fitting that season. Some locations have decorations up at this time that you might be interested in using. In season weddings, people will attire themselves in respective colors. You are not restricted to all the things that come in that season. But you can include a flower that you like from another season.

For Wedding Songs

Music is an immensely powerful element. People believe that the first dance at a wedding is particularly important. Recently many have made a show of it and turned it into an entertainment piece. However, the wedding music you play is especially important. It can kill the vibe of the wedding reception section, or it can get the party started as well as set the pace. You will want to consider a host of different options or genre and cater to all the different guests present. But most importantly you want to select songs you will enjoy and that you will remember as your favorites for years to come.

The most crucial decision is to locate someone who is knowledgeable about wedding music and the selection of music; especially if you are supplying your own music system. Hiring out the job? Then you want a reputable professional, band or group. Ask questions. Have they played at weddings prior? How many? How was the experience? Do they have anyone you can talk to who would refer them? With experience comes an already prepared set of songs or playlists that you can make your selections from.

You should also know when to play music at your wedding, and the appropriate music to play. There are certain times you play a particular type of music. Background wedding music is needed when there are interludes, the processional in addition to the recessional. The same should be when the couple enters at the wedding reception and while the guests are registering. You can do the same when the cake is being cut, when the dance sections starts and for the newlyweds first dance.

The couple should have a hand in deciding the type and tracks played at their wedding. What do you play when the bridal party is going up and down the aisle? Which song will be played for your first dance? Will the bride use the traditional bridal procession? Will you have a choir or use instruments or a pre-recorded CD? If you want to leave a lasting impression, get an excellent and talented singer.

While the guests are partaking in any number of activities you can have lovely background wedding music playing. This should not be loud and jarring but soft and soothing. You can play engaging, and fast paced music when people are dancing, the couple's first dance or while other fun activities are taking place. The first dance song should be incredibly special and a favorite of the newlyweds. The wedding music should make the new married couple enjoy themselves and be proud of hosting a memorable event. Try to be original or unique. You need not follow what others have down but make your own mark.

For Hiring Musicians

There are many details and planning to go through when you are preparing for a wedding. Things like finding the right flowers, in the colors and type that you want and whether you will have to ship them from another country. Also, you must find a caterer who will prepare a delicious menu and has a good record. You must find the perfect wedding gown, and bridesmaid dresses, find a location, get a minister, and decide on rings and vows and finding beautiful invitations. All these preparations and decisions can be tedious, many you will know what to expect before the day of the ceremony. But the wedding music is important, and you may not know until the day of.

Wedding music will set the mood or ambiance of the occasion. The type, genre, pace, and amount of wedding music is your decision. Having instruments such as piano, guitar, flute, harp, or a live band will make the occasion even more memorable and distinct. Your guests will leave having a wonderful time and fun memories. It is a big decision when it comes to selecting musicians or entertainment for your affair. There are many details and questions which should be considered or asked.

You first must think about the type of wedding you want. If you are hosting a casual affair, you may want to reconsider having an orchestra and opera singer. Same for if you are having a very formal affair you might want to rethink having a Pop artiste. Think about whether you want instruments, or tape of live performance with voice. Some people prefer just instrumental music or a classic band. Other might want a wedding musician who is versatile and will mix up the genre of the wedding music to suit the different activities. Ensure you see a performance prior to making your final decision and have a contract in place.

You also must look at the size of your venue. Is it a large hall or a smaller room? This will dictate how many pieces of instruments you need, to ensure that everyone can enjoy the music; but you do not want it too loud in a small setting where it will not sound just as good. To have a solid idea of what you should do, visit the venue first. Ask to see the exact room or location in which the reception or ceremony will be held. If some cases, the ceremony may be held at a church, thereby an organ or instruments may be provided. If not, you should plan accordingly. You may also need to find out from the person in charge of the venue, what type of music is allowed. If this is not in keeping with want you desire to have, you may want to choose a different location. Remember the decision is between both you and your fiancé, so find out what wedding music they like and what they hope to have. Many grooms are quite happy to leave this to their bride's judgment.

For Wedding Speech

Giving speeches or toasts at a wedding is a customary practice. However, finding the appropriate thing to say can be difficult for some people. You do not want to offend anyone or say something not suitable for that setting. There are people who may be overcome by nervousness, but that can be overcome. Preparation will help you be ready to give the perfect wedding speech. Some people find it easier and more helpful to write down their speech or key points on a card. This helps them remember what they want to talk about.

Toasts or weddings speeches should have three parts: an introduction, body, and conclusion. When you decide to tackle writing your speech begin by jointing down a few points or ideas; things you want to include. Make sure it is in some logical or chronological order, so that people are not confused and can follow the thought trend. Leave out anything that is inappropriate or offensive.

Toasts are sometimes a retelling if your experiences with the bride or groom; often funny events that have occurred because of one or the other. Make sure you do not tell any stories that are embarrassing to the bride or groom. You can discuss things about either that no one else knows, but that they would not mind you sharing with the wedding guests and family members. You are also allowed to tell stories about their interests or hobbies. You can get a little bit more creative and include little bits about celebrities or famous people sharing their wedding date or birthday.

Your speech can not be long and winded. Some people give toasts that last forever. This is not only rude but inconsiderate to others who wish to toast and wish the happy couple well. Therefore, it is important to jot down all your points, witty or otherwise and concise them. Stick to the speech. Do not go off course. Guests and the married couple will become annoyed. You do not want to be 'that' person spoken about for years to come. Make it short, sweet, and memorable. Have a funny opening, something that will make them be more responsive to your speech. You can thank the bride and groom for their hospitality and inviting you to the festive occasion. Thank the parents as well.

Your speech should be heard by all; therefore, it cannot be muffled and low. Raise your head and extend your voice. You do not need to shout. Exude confidence, make eye contact, turn, and speak to the wedding party as well as the guests. Look directly at the bride and groom and speak to them in first person; even by calling or using their names. Change the melody, and sound, or volume of your voice so that you do not come off as boring or dull.

Having a wedding toast is a traditional part of weddings. This is where family and friends get to wish the happy couple well and relive, often funny experiences. There are very funny moments to be found when best men, maid of honors, and family members recount their experiences with either the groom or bride. But deciding on who should give toasts at the wedding might be a difficult prospect? It is a long-time practice for men to do the toast, but more and more women are doing toasts. If you have a wedding day coming up and are curious about how to do it, continue reading for more information.

It is so easy to say something that might be misinterpreted by someone else. People look at things differently and you or your friends finding a wedding toast hilarious might be viewed as insensitive or rude to the other family. When coming up with a toast, try to balance this concern, and try to say something that might offend anyone. You will also have to consider the theme or wedding setting. Is it causal, or formal? Is it a stuffy elegant affair or a super cool beach wedding? The more informal the wedding, the easier it is to come up with a toast. One tends to have to be on their best behavior when attending black tie, formal events. You can also get the ear of the happy couple prior and ask questions to see type of toasts they might prefer.

Are you wondering who will give the first wedding toast? Typically, it is the best man. He will lead the way in feeding anecdotes to the wedding guests about the bride and the groom. Sometimes it is difficult being the first, but it is made easier by the relationship that he has with the lovely couple. That is why it is important that when choosing a best man, this person is really a close friend. The best man also has the added responsibility of offering gratitude to the bride and groom's parents. He will express his wishes to them for raising their children and helping them prepare for such an occasion. The final person he should toast is the bride.

The groom will follow the best man and give his wedding toast. He should thank everyone, including the parents, guests, the wedding party, and his lovely bride. It is customary to make mention of the loveliness of the of the bridesmaids and express his gratitude for them helping his bride. His bride should be thrilled by his reference to how they met their journey throughout their relationship and everything that's happened, in brief, up to the wedding day. Here he will have a chance to be funny, or very sentimental; of course, soliciting tears from his new wife. The bride's father would then proceed with his toast of welcoming family and friends and reflecting on memories of his daughter. Other family and friends can follow if they wish.

For Hosting Out of Town Guests

Weddings are momentous occasions. People travel from near and far to take part in the festivities. For many this is the rare occasion they get to see loved ones and old friends from their past. What do you do with wedding guests? How do you prepare for persons who are travelling from out of town? These are some of the things you must consider when planning a wedding. You should always be very considerate and helpful to people who are travelling great distances to spend that special day with you.

The wedding date is the first thing you need to communicate with them. When planning or selecting a wedding date it is good to give your guests adequate notice. This allows them to prepare, save and buy any relevant items. Travel expenses can be extremely high, and they may need some time to get this together. Sending the invitation with short notice would not be fair to them. You can also do follow up calls, to ensure that all is well with them, and that they are having no difficulties, in getting accommodation or transportation.

Children are also a concern. When you invite friends or family, think about their children; especially if they are younger. Be prepared to include them in the guests list if they have no one to take care of or watch them. If children are not allowed at the reception, you can have a babysitting service provided for them.

Having websites, emails, or Facebook pages with constant updates on wedding plans is a novel idea and effective way to keep people informed. You can post a lot of interesting information here. This can include places to stay like inns and hotels. You can also discuss things to do, like parks, festivals or shows. Of importance might be directions, maps and flight or weather advisories. Your guests will be incredibly grateful for the extra assistance. Many of your guests might want to know how your wedding plans are going, and how they can help if you are having any difficulties. This is also a way in which you will have memories that last. People will make their comments and suggestions, and you can use these same mediums to post pictures and give updates after the wedding is over.

Closer to the wedding you may not have the time, to do all the things mentioned before. You will be caught up in last minute arrangements and your own personal planning. This is where you need to have someone else who will monitor emails, update pages, and send advisories. Ensure your guests update or send you their contact information, such as cell phone numbers and email addresses. You should intern contacts for them as well. This should be with persons who are aware of your efforts or the same set or persons who sent out advisories.

When they get to the wedding, ensure to spend a little time with them. After all they travelled a wonderful way to see you. Talk about old times and catch up on what's been happening in their lives. They will appreciate this, especially because of the importance of the occasion and how busy you will be. You can also make it easy for them by assisting with accommodation arrangement. If your venue has rooms for guests, you can get a package deal. Find out from in town friends and family if they have rooms available.

For Guest Attire

Everyone loves to dress up and try on different outfits. Some people may even have a personal style or preference for wearing certain colors like tan, browns, and blacks. Others tend to be more outgoing and have pinks, purples, or blues only, in their wardrobe. Wearing the appropriate color to an event is especially important. Colors evoke a certain mood. They are also representative of respect at events. Parties, weddings, and funerals have a tradition of colors that are worn to them. However, weddings are not events where you will wear black, unless explicit requested by the bride. Nor are funerals places you will wear bright shocking-colored outfits. These events demand you respect the ceremony, the occasion, and the people there.

Wearing black to an event like a wedding is unsuitable for a lot of reasons. The primary reason is that the person who does this is going against tradition. People can have their personal preference and style, however being unique at a wedding is not the thing to do. Weddings may represent a show of traditional beliefs and not about being practical. The fact that a wedding is an example of a ceremony refers to tradition and honoring tradition. It may also be considered inconsiderate or disrespectful. Trying to be unique and not respecting the tradition of others.

You also do not want to draw attention away from the bride and groom. A wedding is about the couple and their commitment to each other; it is not about the costumes worn by their guests. Furthermore, you can rest assured that they will not appreciate anyone taking the focus and the special meaning away. Therefore, do not wear black to a wedding.

Continuing with the reasons not to wear black to a wedding; many believe that it is in poor taste to wear black to a wedding. The color is accepted as being best suited for a formal event. It might be acceptable if the wedding is a formal evening event. Regarding fashion, it would be considered a fashion faux pas. The mood set at any event wedding, funeral or a party is largely influenced by the ambience, and ambience by color. Black does not invite a feeling of happiness, love, and excitement at a wedding. It is reminiscent of authority, power, grief, or death. Colors that evoke joy, love and warmth are more preferred for the wedding scene.

The colors worn to any event is important and has meaning. Black is not a color to be worn at weddings unless it is a formal evening event. Consideration should be given to the whole purpose or reason of a wedding and attendees should not be selfish and try to draw attention to themselves. Being seen as distracting is never good of wanted at a wedding unless you are the one getting married.

Getting married is supposed to be a joyous occasion, filled with good tidings from family members and friends. This milestone marks the point in your life where you will select the person you want to be with forever; or so they say. For some it is a very intimidating and stressful event, while for others fully certain of their decision it is encapsulated with happiness and bliss. Weddings are some of the biggest events in any person's lifetime. The planning and effort that goes into this ceremony often takes month to do. As a result, one must be very certain that the person you say yes to is the one, you want to spend your life with forever.

Many brides or grooms leave the other standing at the altar or changing their minds at the last minute. Not only reeking embarrassment on their jilted fiancé, but also on the families. The attendees at a wedding are often close friends and family and important associates of the family; therefore, living down the embarrassment will be next to impossible. Often with occurrences like that, many families have dissension and a split in the family unit. Parents might end up resenting the actions of their children and withdraw their support to them. Also being left with a hefty bill, adds salt to the wound. Weddings take a lot of planning and financial investment. Time is spent by almost all involved with the family to make is a success. Choosing caterers, cake, wine, menu, flowers, location, gowns, and many other details that go into launching this event is an emotional as well as financial investment. Therefore, to throw all that away is considered coldblooded and malicious.

The movie runaway bride starring Julia Roberts is a perfect example of a person waiting until the last minute to decide that their partner is not the best to suit them. Couples need to be one hundred percent certain before they start planning a wedding. Planning a wedding can be an intoxicating experience, and many people get married specially to do this. But if you have doubts address them before the big day. Couple's counselling is often recommended before tying the knot. This allows both the bride and groom to be, to discuss concerns they may have. It also serves to make them aware of what a marriage really is and the work it will take to make it successful. Many couples really begin to understand who their partner is and what they expect out of a marriage in the counselling session. Pastors or counsellors are objective parties who will give advice and make unbiased recommendations. If you still have doubts after this, you should not get married.

Weddings do not normally go how we plan. There are many things that may happen in between before that time or even on the date to cause your plans to go awry. Brides or grooms change their minds, cancelling the ceremony, eloping or dates being moved up for family emergencies. Sometimes, nature makes the decision for us, when storms are coming, and dates must be either moved up or down. You must have an open mind and see the importance of the occasion to genuinely enjoy it, whenever it does happen and not be stressed out.

One bride has been waiting to get married for many years. Her mother has been planning ever since she was eighteen, trying to find doctors, professionals and when she got older anyone who would marry her. This might sound hilarious, but t her it was stressful. Eventually she got engaged, and her mother went into wedding planning overdrive. The groom had not yet bought rings before the mother had invitations, entertainment, cake, and location planned. Though the couple wanted a small intimate affair, the bride's mother was going for the event of the decade.

The wedding was eventually cancelled due to the groom's mother becoming gravely ill. They had only days to change the plans and bring the wedding to wherever the groom's mother was going to be. This is exceedingly difficult to do when your fiancé's mother is dying, and his father is losing his life partner. All the previous plans and down payments were lost. No refunds. Invitations were now readjusted, to emails and paper. Bridesmaids were disgruntled and the location would be three states away. Then add to all that trying to find venues in that area, and a restaurant that can accommodate guests on short notice, not too far from the hospital. Then, a few days before all this was to be executed his mom grew even more serious and sickly. The wedding had to be held at the hospital, with no guests but the nurses as witnesses and bridesmaids, the groom, and the parents. There was no music or speeches, just the love of family.

There was a photographer who had his skills assessed, doing calisthenics trying to keep up with a bride, who also forgot her shoes and had to run the hospital halls just to locate them. The nurses prepared the grooms mother, washed her hair, and made her up nicely. Many hospital rules were broken that day, but the ceremony was lovely. Nothing else mattered to the newlyweds. All in attendance were crying and the groom's parents had tears in their eyes, holding hands. The pictures from the wedding will show the love and joy from that day. The groom's mother died shortly after and his father as well. In life we must remember what is important and not be caught up in the trivialities of things. Weddings are an important occasion, but they mean even more when shared with family and friends.

People make mistakes and many do not have the best of memories. On the wedding day, you may have to trust people with particularly important assignments, like taking the wedding rings. If the best man, forgets where he left the wedding ring, simply borrow those of your parents, family members of close friends. Some might even boast about it afterwards. You can strangle the best man after the ceremony. All brides have a constant dread that their makeup will start running. Some do not care and will cry torrents, but for those who do care, wear water and smudge proof cosmetics. If you have a makeup artist, ensure they are on the guests list and standing close by.

Spot removers aren't just used on everyday clothes stains; they are good for short notice and immediate use as well. Having your wedding gown or suit messed up or stained can be a major distraction from the fun and festivities around you; brides especially become so distracted and start to think everyone is talking about it. But you can prepare from something happening by taking along a spot removal kit.

Watching a wedding cake melt due to heat does not make for a happy couple; especially if the cake falls. This can leave the married couple broken hearted, especially the bride. Cutting of the cake has been a tradition passed on for generations and many spend months trying to locate and choose the best tasting wedding cake. If possible, have your cake stored in a cool place or a fridge; this should cut down the amount of time spent in the heat, between being taken to the venue and being cut. Bring it out about ten or five minutes before the cutting of the cake part of the reception. You should also have the cake team carry a repair kit, which most professional cake makers typically do.

If more people turn up at the reception than who were invited, you should ensure that extra chairs are available. Therefore, contacting everyone who haven't RSVP, two weeks prior, will save on the stress caused from this. Leave a margin of about five to ten on your guests list. Also, to avoid getting bad pictures, get a professional photographer and videographer. Do not be cheap; these images capture your memories for years to come.

Weddings, when planned correctly and all contingencies put in place are typically beautiful affairs. However, sometimes things go so horribly wrong, that though some are unavoidable others you just did not see coming. One thing that many people often pray for on their wedding day is clear and sunny skies; but rain can be a damper, though it is unavoidable. You can minimize this inconvenience by having your wedding during the dry, sunny months. Also, check whether forecasts. You can rent tents if you plan to have your wedding in an outdoor environment. When choosing your location, check if they have contingencies or an indoor setting if rain decides to fall that day. The key to avoiding disasters is to make lists, start planning from early, make alternative plans and hire experienced professionals when possible.

Weddings can either be complex or simple, depending on any number of factors. First, the wedding ceremony usually includes an introduction or statement from the minister or officiating minister. Of course, the giving away of the bride and sometime the question of whether anyone objects to the union. These are standard inclusions in every wedding ceremony. However, these will vary somewhat depending on the type of wedding ceremony, the religious beliefs, and other personal preferences.

Beyond those inclusions, couples tend to include everything from chants, poetry readings, musical interludes, singing, bible readings and many other variations. After all this, the couple will begin to recite their wedding vows; promising to love, cherish and be faithful to each other. Some religions or denominations allow you to vary the wedding vows as you see fit, while keeping the general message.

It is important to think about and read through the vows before you say them. This will enlighten both the bride and the groom in what they are promising each other. Sometimes this may be done in couples counselling or in meeting the person who will host the ceremony. Many marriages are ending in divorce, more so now than ever. Therefore, you and your future spouse must understand that it takes work and that it will not be perfect every day. You will both have a difference in opinion on many occasions, do things to hurt the other person, or simply have shortcomings that are difficult for your spouse to live with. Therefore, spend time communicating, asking questions, observing, and even getting couples counselling before the big day. This will create a strong foundation for your relationship, and you will be less likely to have wedding day jitters, cold feet, or divorce soon after marrying your partner. You will be 100% certain when you exchange vows.

Some ceremonies have the lighting of a unity candle after the exchange of wedding vows, while others that are more traditional, have the exchange of rings. More modern ceremonies have the releasing of doves, other birds, or butterflies; some may have a musical rendition. For some people, the most important part, is the pronouncement of the couple being husband and wife, and the kiss. A blessing would have been said over the wedding couple just before this part of the ceremony. These parts are what a wedding ceremony is all about and should never be forgotten or taken lightly.

Remember, you must contact the Ministry of National Security & Justice at least four weeks prior to having your Jamaican wedding getaway. This allows you to arrange for a marriage license that will permit you to legally have your ceremony on the island. The cost may vary.

Contact the Ministry anytime during the week between normal business hours. You will need proper documentation to assist in getting your marriage certificate. Birth certificates, divorce papers, death certificates, all these are required if applicable, to prove that you are legally single and above the age of consent to marry. Once, this process is complete, you can freely continue with your Jamaican wedding plans.

Having a checklist is recommended because they help to keep us organised. It is essential in the preparation process and minimises any potential problems later. Use this checklist to avoid stress and keep track of all the wedding plans and details.

Wedding Categories List

Category	Group
Alterations	Attire
Bride	Attire
Groom	Attire
Aisle Runner	Ceremony
Chair Rental	Ceremony
Flowers	Ceremony
Gratuity	Ceremony
Musicians	Ceremony
Officiant / Clergy	Ceremony
Other	Ceremony
Other Decor	Ceremony
Transportation to Reception	Ceremony
Ushers	Ceremony
Accommodations	Honeymoon
Airfare	Honeymoon

Category	Group
Entertainment	Honeymoon
Meals	Honeymoon
Rental Car	Honeymoon
Engagement Photos	Photo and Video
Photo Albums	Photo and Video
Videography	Photo and Video
Wedding Photos	Photo and Video
Additional Transportation	Reception
Bartender	Reception
Catering	Reception
Chairs	Reception
Decorations	Reception
Dishes	Reception
Gratuities	Reception
Guest Book	Reception
Linens	Reception
Liquor / Beverages	Reception
Misc	Reception
Musicians / DJ	Reception
Sound / Lighting	Reception
Tables	Reception
Tent / Rental Setup	Reception
Venue Fee	Reception
Wedding Cake	Reception
Bartender / Beverages	Rehearsal Dinner
Food / Catering	Rehearsal Dinner
Music	Rehearsal Dinner
Rentals and Misc	Rehearsal Dinner
Engagement Ring	Rings

Category	Group
Engraving	Rings
Wedding Bands	Rings
Address Labels	Stationary
Invitations	Stationary
Postage	Stationary
Save the Date Cards	Stationary
Thank You Notes	Stationary
Wedding Programs	Stationary
Gifts	Wedding Savings
Our Contribution	Wedding Savings
Parents	Wedding Savings

Wedding Checklist

	WEDDING CHECKLIST
√	**1 year to 10 months before**
	Decide on a budget.
	Choose a date or a timeframe.
	Locate your venue.
	Find a wedding planner, florist, photographer, videographer, caterer and a DJ or a band.
	Find a hotel and reserve room blocks.
	Hire a professional for save-the-dates and wedding invitations.
	Decide on the members of your wedding party.
	Read. Research. Get informed.

	WEDDING CHECKLIST
	Shop for the wedding dress.
√	**9-7 mths before**
	Decide on an officiant, like a pastor, close friend or other professional. Ensure they are licensed.
	Research the policy for marriage licenses where you are getting married.
	Choose your bridesmaids' dresses and grooms men suits.
	Start looking for a hair and makeup stylist.
	Start planning the rehearsal dinner.
	Contact event rentals and place your order.
	For destination weddings, book your tickets and start making travel plans.
	Organize air, bus, or car transportation.
√	**6-4 mths before**
	Arrange for wedding cake tasting and make an order.
	Confirm wedding colors and attire.
	Confirm addresses and start sending out wedding invitations.
	Decide on wedding favors.
	Commence working on ceremony details such as programs, and signage.
	Select ceremony music. Songs you will walk up, and down the aisle to as well as for your first dance as a married couple.
√	**3-2 mths before**
	Draft your wedding vows.

	WEDDING CHECKLIST
	Get wedding RSVPs.
	Decide on a treat for the bridal party. This can be a spa day or a luncheon.
	Wrap up your wedding songs list.
√	**1 mth before**
	Follow up on RSVPs and confirm guests.
	Prepare seating chart and cards.
	Get your bridal shoes and test it out before the wedding day.
	Collect all wedding day paper materials.
	Verify you have your marriage license. Keep this in a safe place.
	Locate and confirm childcare, babysitters, pet sitters and house sitters if needed; especially if you will be gone on a long honeymoon.
√	**1-2 weeks before**
	Conduct final confirmation with all vendors, caterers, etc. Advise them of the adjusted guest count.
	Collect your wedding dress and tuxedo.
	Arrange gratuity.
	Get cash and correct currency for travel destination.
	Touchbase with all the bridesmaids and groomsmen. Notify them of any expectations.
	Check for weather updates and plan accordingly.
	Pack your bags.
	Double check travel arrangements

	Check in with your partner, spend time together and discuss any last-minute details.
	Rest and Relax.

Wedding Budget List

Category	Estimated Cost	Actual Cost
Alterations		
Bride		
Groom		
Aisle Runner		
Chair Rental		
Flowers		
Gratuity		
Musicians		
Officiant / Clergy		
Decor		
Transportation to Reception		
Ushers		
Accommodations		
Airfare		
Entertainment		
Meals		
Rental Car		
Engagement Photos		
Photo Albums		

Videography		
Wedding Photos		
Additional Transportation		
Bartender		
Catering		
Chairs		
Decorations		
Dishes		
Gratuities		
Guest Book		
Linens		
Liquor / Beverages		
Miscellaneous		
Musicians / DJ		
Sound / Lighting		
Tables		
Tent / Rental Setup		
Venue Fee		
Wedding Cake		
Bartender / Beverages		
Food / Catering		
Music		
Rentals and Misc		
Engagement Ring		
Engraving		
Wedding Bands		
Address Labels		
Invitations		

Postage		
Save the Date Cards		
Thank You Notes		
Wedding Programs		
Gifts		
Parents		
Other		
Other		

Wedding Guests List

Guests Names	Address	Contact Numbers

Wedding Vendors List

Vendor Names	Address	Contact Numbers	Email
Pastor/Officiant			
Wedding Coordinator			
Caterer			
Photographer			
Videographer			
Barber			
Hair Stylist			
Makeup			
Wedding dress			
Groom's/Tux			
Wedding cake			
Florist			
DJ or Band			
Stationer / Graphic Designer			
Jeweler			
Wedding favors vendor			
Rentals company			
Transportation Company			
Airline			
Hotel			
Rental Car Agency			
Venue			

Water-locked, river-a-plenty, and mountainous; Jamaica is one of the most beautiful Caribbean countries. It is envied for more than its sand, sea, and surf. This jewel has provided the ideal locations for couples who want to celebrate an important and memorable day in their lives. Jamaican weddings are typically gorgeous and there are numerous spots on the island where thousands of couples have celebrated their nuptials in paradise.

This island haven is also called home by some of the most talented and creative people in the world, brimming with culture and native beauty. Jamaicans are widely described as friendly and engaging and our music is world-renowned. Say the name, Bob Marley anywhere on this planet. Speak the patois or even utter the name Usain Bolt and everyone knows it's Jamaica. For a little island, Jamaica has a big personality and has a lot to offer.

Then, there is the warm Caribbean sun and sexy white and black sand beaches. Jamaica is paradise for many, no wonder so many tourists flock to its shores every year. The north coast is the preferred playground for most visitors from all over the world; America, Europe, South America, and England, are just a few countries with high visitor rates. Moreover, tourism is the biggest income earner; millions of people have vacationed, visited, lymed, gotten married, and honeymooned on the Reggae Island.

Weddings are momentous events in everyone's lives. It joins families together forever and provides happy memories that will be cherished for an eternity. Jamaica specializes in creating these memories and that's why it is ranked as one of the top wedding destinations for tying the knot, jumping the broom, or getting hitched, every year.

With its diverse culture, couples have many options to choose from. Those choices vary from traditional to contemporary; at a church or on the beach, in the garden or in a gorgeously decorated hotel space. Couples have the option of having a low-key affair or an event to rival the most exclusive of celebrity social functions; whatever the happy couple wants, the happy couple gets.

The tongue seeks to be pleasured on the wedding day and only the most exquisite, succulent, and savory foods will satisfy its demand. When it comes to preparing the most delectable of meals, the chefs in Jamaica are second to none. Keeping the couple happy is always the main priority and the cooks will ensure this by preparing the best cuisines at the wedding reception. Couples will be enchanted with a wide array of spices, recipes, and liqueurs.

Jamaican caterers, chefs and cooks are also talented artisans when it comes to creating delicacies. Their main goal is to create meals that you and your spouse will never forget. To the extent that you will return every year on your honeymoon just to recapture those happy memories and those tempting tastes and aromas. Couples will have the option to enjoy local dishes such as fried, barbeque and jerk chicken, ackee and salt fish or dishes from your native home. Prepare to have your guests shower you with compliments and commendations, as your reception menu will be filled with mouthwatering delicacies.

Considered the center piece of every wedding, the cake will be beautiful, elegant, memorable, unique, delicious and worth every dollar. Wedding cakes will vary depending on your preference. Please feel free to request inventive and futuristic designs as our bakers will work relentlessly to fashion whatever you request.

Remember, Jamaica is a popular destination for many couples who want to get married. Countless hotels cater to this kind of event that brings brides and grooms to the island seeking the ultimate experience. They assist with planning many of the intricate details involved in hosting the event. From accommodation, location, church, reception, food, flowers, and the honeymoon; you name it, they got it covered. Planning a wedding getaway? Do you want to know what to do? Chose Jamaica and prepare for a memorable experience.

There is much that Jamaica has to offer, hotels, beaches, rivers, food and so much more. Below you will find listings of all these.

Map of Jamaica

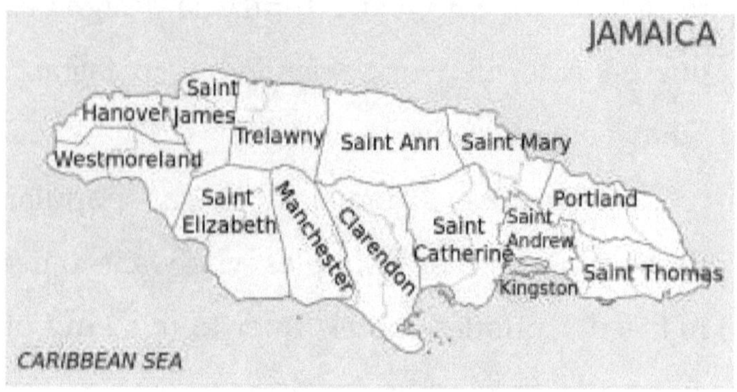

Hotels in Jamaica

Falmouth/Trelawny

1. Breezes Resort & Spa Trelawny

2. FDR Pebbles Hotel

3. Gloustershire Hotel

4. Grand Lido Braco Spa & Resort

5. Pebbles Resort

6. Retreat Guesthouse Luxury Suites

7. Starfish Trelawny Beach Resort

Kingston and St. Andrew

1. Altamont Court Hotel

2. Christar Villas

3. Courtleigh Hotel

4. Forres Park Nature Resort and Spa

5. Four Seasons Hotel

6. Goblin Hill Villas

7. Hilton Hotel

8. Indies Hotel

9. Jamaica Pegasus Hotel

10. Knutsford Court Hotel

11. Mayfair Hotel

12. Morgan's Harbour Hotel

13. Oceana Hotel

14. Sandhurst Hotel

15. Strawberry Hill Hotel

16. Sutton Place Hotel

17. Terra Nova Hotel

18. The Spanish Court Hotel

Montego Bay/St. James

1. Blue Harbour Hotel
2. Breezes Hotel
3. Buccaneer Beach Hotel
4. Castles by the Sea Hotel
5. Coral Cliff Hotel and Entertainment Resort
6. Couples Secret Rendezvous Hotel
7. Coyaba Beach Resort
8. Doctors Cave Beach Hotel
9. El Greco Resort
10. Emeraldview Resort Villa
11. Gloustershire Hotel
12. Gran Bahia Principe Jamaica Hotel
13. Grand Lido Braco Hotel
14. Grand Palladium Lady Hamilton Resort and Spa
15. Half Moon Club Hotel
16. Half Moon Royal Villas
17. Holiday Inn Sunspree Resort
18. Iberostar Rose Hall Beach Hotel

19. Iberostar Rose Hall Suites

20. Iberostar Grand Hotel

21. On Top of the World Villa Hotel

22. Paradise Montego Bay Villas Resort

23. Pebbles Hotel

24. Relax Resort

25. Richmond Hill Hotel

26. Ritz-Carlton Rose Hall Resort

27. Rose Hall Castles Beach Resort

28. Rose Hall Resort and Country Club

29. Round Hill Villas and Hotel

30. Royal Decameron Beach Hotel

31. Sandals All Inclusive

32. Sandals Euro

33. Sandals Inn

34. Sandals Royal Caribbean Resort

35. Secrets Wild Orchid Hotel

36. Sunset Beach Resort & Spa

37. SuperClubs Super Surprise Hotel

38. Toby's Resort

39. Wexford Court Hotel

Negril/Hanover

1. Bar B Barn Hotel
2. Beach Club Condos
3. Beach Club Condo's
4. Beach Comber Club Hotel
5. Beach House Villas
6. Beaches All Inclusive Resort
7. Beaches Sandy Bay
8. Beaches Spa and Resort
9. Bungalow Hotel
10. Caribbean Sunset Resort
11. Carib Beach Apartments
12. Catcha Falling Star Resort
13. Catchafallingstar Hotel
14. Caves Hotel
15. Charela Inn
16. CocoLaPalm Seaside Resort
17. Coral Cove Resort
18. Coral Seas Cliff Resort
19. Coral Seas Garden Resort
20. Coral Seas Spa & Beach Resort

21. Country Country Beach Cottages

22. Couples Hotel

23. Couples Swept Away Hotel

24. Escape Resort

25. Firefly Beach Cottages

26. Foote Prints on the Sands Hotel

27. Fun Holiday Beach Resort

28. Golden Sunset Hotel

29. Grand Lido Resort

30. Hedonism II Resort

31. Home Sweet Home Seaside Resort

32. Idle Awhile Resort

33. La Mar Cafe and Resort

34. Legends Beach Resort

35. Lost Beach Resort

36. Merrill's Beach Resort

37. Negril Gardens Resort

38. Palm Beach Club Hotel

39. Paradise View Hotel

40. Point Village Resort

41. Rhodes Hall Plantation

42. Riu All Inclusive Club Hotel

43. Riu Tropical Bay Resort

44. Rocalta Spa & Resort

45. Rockhouse Hotel

46. Rondel Village

47. Samsara Hotel

48. Sandals Beach Resort

49. Sandy Bay Beaches Hotel

50. Sandy Haven Resort

51. Sea Splash Resort

52. Seasplash Resort

53. Secrets Cabins Beach Hotel

54. Shields Villas

55. Sunrise Club

56. Sunset at the Palms Resort

57. Sunset Caribbean Hotel

58. Sunset Hotel

59. Swept Away Resort

60. Tensing Pen Hotel

61. The Inn

62. Thrills Resort

63. Travellers Beach Resort Hotel

64. Tree House Cottages

65. Tree House Resort

66. Villa La Cage

67. Whistling Bird Resort

68. White Sands Hotel

Ocho Rios/St. Ann

1. Braco Village Hotel & Spa

2. Beaches Boscobel Resort

3. Breezes Hotel

4. Cardiff Hotel and Spa

5. Chrisanns Beach Resort

6. Club Ambiance Resort

7. Club Ambience

8. Columbus Heights Jamaica Hotel

9. Couples Ocho Rios Hotel

10. Couples Sans Souci Resort

11. Crane Ridge Resort

12. Crane Ridge Suites

13. Crystal Ripple Beach Lodge

14. Del Mar Villa

15. Fisherman's Point Resort

16. Franklyn D Resort

17. Goldeneye Hotel

18. Gran Bahia Principe Jamaica Hotel

19. Grand Lido Braco Resort

20. Grande Sport Villa Golf Resort

21. Hedonism III Resort

22. High Hope Estate Hotel

23. Jamaica Inn

24. Jewel Dunn's River Beach Resort and Spa

25. Jewel Runaway Bay Beach & Golf Resort

26. Jewel Paradise Cove Beach Resort & Spa

27. Mystic Ridge Resort

28. Paradise L Horizon Villas

29. Riu Ocho Rios Hotel

30. Rooms on the Beach Hotel

31. Royal Decameron Fun Beach Resort &
    Spa

32. Royal Plantation Spa & Hotel

33. Runaway Bay Alamanda Inn

34. Runaway Bay Breezes Resort

35. Runaway Bay Heart Hotel

36. Sandals Dunn's River Golf Resort &
    Spa

37. Sandals Dunn's River Villaggio Resort
    Hotel

38. Sandals Grande Riviera Beach & Villa
    Golf Resort

39. Sandals Royal Plantation

40. Sandcastles Resort

41. Shaw Park Beach Hotel

42. Silver Seas Hotel

43. Sky Castles Hotel

44. Sunflower Beach Resort and Villas

45. Sunflower Runaway Bay Beach Resort

46. Sunset Jamaica Grande Resort

47. Village Hotel in Ocho Rios

Port Antonio/Portland

1. Jamaica Palace Hotel

2. Mockingbird Hill

3. Robins Bay Village & Beach Resort St. Mary

St. Elizabeth

1. Jakes Hotel

2. Marblue Hotel

3. Sandals Whitehouse Hotel

4. Treasure Beach Hotel

Beaches in Jamaica

On the North Coast

1. Cardiff Hall Public Beach in St. Ann
2. Dunns River Beach in St. Ann
3. Puerto Seco Beach in St. Ann
4. Reggae Vibes Beach in St. Ann
5. Turtle Beach in St. Ann
6. Burwood Beach in Trelawny
7. Duncan's Bay Beach in Trelawny
8. Silver Sands beach in Trelawny
9. Cornwall Beach in Montego Bay
10. Doctor's Cave Beach in Montego Bay
11. Rose Hall Beach Club in Montego Bay
12. Walter Fletcher Beach / Aquasol Beach and Theme Park in Montego Bay

On the West Coast

1. Seven mile long, Negril Beach
2. Cosmos Beach in Hanover
3. Auchindown Beach in Westmoreland

4. Bluefields Beach in Westmoreland

5. Belmont Beach in Westmoreland

6. Whitehouse Beach in Westmoreland

On the South Coast

1. Alligator Pond in Manchester

2. Billys Bay in St. Elizabeth

3. Calabash Bay in St. Elizabeth

4. Crane Road Beach in St. Elizabeth

5. Font Hill Beach in St. Elizabeth

6. Great Pedro Bay in St. Elizabeth

7. Treasure Beach in St. Elizabeth

On the East Coast

1. James Bond Beach in St. Mary

2. Strawberry Fields in St. Mary

3. Boston Beach in Portland

4. Ennises Bay Beach in Portland

5. Fairy Hill Beach in Portland

6. Frenchman's Cove in Portland

7. Long Bay Beach in Portland

8.   San San beach in Portland

9.   Winifred Beach in Portland

10. Holland Bay in St. Thomas

11. Prospect Beach in St. Thomas

12. Swimmers Bay Beach in St. Thomas

13. Under the Rock Beach in St. Thomas

14. Lime Cay off the coast of Kingston

15. Gunboat Beach in Kingston

16. Hellshire Beach in St. Catherine

17. Sugarman's Beach in St. Catherine

18. Rafter's Nest Beach

Rivers in Jamaica

On the North Coast

1. White River in St. Ann
2. Martha Brae River in Trelawny
3. Great River in St. James
4. Montego River in St. James

On the West Coast

1. Lucea East River in Hanover
2. Lucea West River in Hanover
3. Cabarita River in Westmoreland
4. Dean's River in Westmoreland
5. Negril River in Westmoreland

On the South Coast

1. Black River in St. Elizabeth
2. Milk River in Clarendon
3. Rio Minho in Clarendon
4. Rio Cobre in St. Catherine

On the East Coast

1. Hope River in St. Andrew

2. Morant River in St. Thomas

3. Plantain Garden River in St. Thomas

4. Yallahs River in St. Thomas

5. Buff Bay River in Portland

6. Hector's River   in Portland

7. Rio Grande in Portland

8. Rio Nueve in St. Mary

9. Wag Water River in St. Mary

Foods in Jamaica

Fruits

1. Banana
2. Blue mountain coffee
3. Cashew
4. Cherry
5. Coconut
6. Custard apple
7. Guava
8. Guinep
9. Jackfruit
10. Jelly coconut
11. June plum
12. Lime
13. Mammey apple
14. Mango
15. Melon
16. Naseberry
17. Nutmeg
18. Ortanique

19. Otaheite apple

20. Papaya

21. Passion fruit

22. Pear

23. Soursop

24. Star apple

25. Sugar cane

26. Sweetsop

27. Tamarind

Porridge

1. Banana porridge

2. Cornmeal porridge

3. Hominy corn porridge

4. Oats porridge

5. Plantain porridge

6. Rice porridge

7. Peanut porridge

Soups

1. Chicken soup

2. Beef soup

3. Callaloo soup

4. Cucumber soup

5. Fish tea

6. Green peas soup

7. Gungo peas soup

8. Pepper pot soup

9. Manish water soup

10. Pumpkin soup

11. Red peas soup

Meats

1. Ackee and saltfish

2. Baked chicken

3. Coconut chicken

4. Conch

5. Cow foot

6. Curried chicken

7. Curried goat

8. Curried lobster

9. Curried shrimp

10. Escovitch fish

11. Fried chicken

12. Jerk chicken

13. Jerk fish

14. Jerk lobster

15. Jerk pork

16. Jerk sausage

17. Mackerel run down

18. Meatballs

19. Oxtail

20. Roast beef

21. Roast chicken

22. Seafood

23. Steamed fish

24. Stew peas

25. Stewed beef

26. Stewed chicken

Sides

1. Rice and peas

2. Callaloo rice

3. Pumpkin rice

4. Spanish rice

5. Ackee rice

6. Boiled dumplings

7. Fried dumplings

8. Boiled plantains

9. Fried plantains

10. Boiled green bananas

11. Boiled potatoes

12. Mashed potatoes

13. Boiled breadfruit

14. Roast breadfruit

15. Fried breadfruit

16. Sweet potatoes

17. Yam

18. Cassava

19. Dasheen

20. Callaloo

21. Carrot

22. Cabbage and calloo

23. Corn beef and cabbage

24. Steamed cabbage

25. Bammy

26. Festival

27. Saltfish fritters

28. Tripe and beans

Cakes

1. Rum cake or Christmas cake

2. Pineapple upside-down cake

3. Sponge cake

4. Carrot cake

5. Cheesecake

6. Banana cake

7. Black forest cake

8. Chocolate cake

9. Coffee cake

Pastry

1. Apple pie

2. Banana bread

3. Banana fritters

4. Beef patty

5. Blue draws

6. Bread pudding

7. Brownie

8. Bulla

9. Chicken patty

10. Coco bread

11. Coconut drops

12. Coconut gizzada

13. Corn bread

14. Cornmeal pudding

15. Grater cake

16. Guava cheese

17. Jackass corn

18. Meatloaf

19. Plantain tarts

20. Spice bun

21. Sweet potato pudding

22. Tamarind balls

23. Toto

Spices and Herbs

1. Cerasee
2. Country pepper
3. Ginger
4. Nutmeg
5. Pimento
6. Scallion (escallion)
7. Scotch bonnet pepper
8. Sorrel
9. Thyme
10. Vanilla

Remember, you must contact the Ministry of National Security & Justice at least four weeks prior to having your Jamaican wedding getaway. This allows you to arrange for a marriage license that will permit you to legally have your ceremony on the island. The cost may vary. Contact the Ministry anytime during the week between normal business hours. You will need proper documentation to assist in getting your marriage certificate. Birth certificates, divorce papers, death certificates, all these are required if applicable, to prove that you are legally single and above the age of consent to marry. Once, this process is complete, you can freely continue with your Jamaican wedding plans.

Acknowledgment

There is one source of wisdom. There is one source of passion. There is one source of strength. There is one source of motivation. There is one source of drive and there is one source from where every dream, vision, and gift flows; that source is God. Without him, none of this would be possible. It is His guidance, vision, and urging that has made all this possible; the book, Jamaica Pen Publishers, and the dreams from which they came. I honor Him.

To my support, my twin. You are the oil in my engine, the fire in my heart, the meaning of everything, and the answer to why. I thank you for your encouragement, patience, counsel, and your prayers.

- *Denise N. Fyffe*

Jamaica Pen Publisher's principal author, Denise N. Fyffe, is no stranger  to producing books. She has written more than 50 books and continues to inspire new authors through our mentorship program.

Fyffe, as she is often called, grew up in Jamaica and pursued a career in Education, Training, and Software Implementation. A lifelong scholar, Denise often releases educational and nonfiction content.

Some of her previous works include Treasures of Colombia, The Caribbean Family, How to Keep Writing, and The Philosophy of Education and Work. Her latest release is Treasures of Jamaica, a follow-up to Treasures of Colombia, which she produced in collaboration with a co-author. That book also highlighted traditional foods, but from Colombia.

Read more about Denise N. Fyffe on our website at:

https://jamaicapenpublishers.com/.

The Island Journal

This book shares various aspects of the Jamaican
culture, music, and lifestyle.

Jamaican Pebbles

Poetic expressions and gems of wisdom about nature,
life, love, social issues, and the spiritual.

Recount Jamaica

Recount Jamaica shares poetic verse about my island
home, a review of experiences in years past, including
the good, the bad, and the beautiful.

Treasures of Jamaica

This book shares tasty cuisine and recipes from
Jamaica; from fried dumplings to ackee and saltfish,
and stewed fish to oxtails and butter beans.

How to Keep Writing

This book shares key practical strategies on how to
become an author and a working writer. It helps you to
overcome the everyday nuisances and distractions that
hinder the writing process.

Fibroids: The Alien Assassins in My Body

This book highlights one woman's experience of
fighting this disease over the years. She also includes
details about her surgery and recovery.

Jamaica Pen Publishers
A HELPFUL, HOPEFUL AND HOLISTIC APPROACH
TO DIGITAL PUBLISHING